The
DECLARATION
of
INDEPENDENCE
The Evolution of the Text

By Julian P. Boyd
Edited by Gerard W. Gawalt

REVISED EDITION

THE LIBRARY OF CONGRESS
in association with the
THOMAS JEFFERSON MEMORIAL FOUNDATION, INC.
Washington and Charlottesville

Distributed by University Press of New England
Hanover and London
1999

Library of Congress Cataloging-in-Publication Data

Boyd, Julian P. (Julian Parks). 1903–
    The Declaration of Independence : the evolution of the text / by
Julian P. Boyd : edited by Gerard W. Gawalt. — Rev. ed.
        p. cm.
    Includes bibliographical references.
    ISBN 0-8444-0980-4 (alk. paper)
    1. United States. Declaration of Independence—Criticism.
Textual. I. Gawalt. Gerard W. II. Title.
E221.B69 1999
973.3'13—dc21

                                                                98-54837
                                                                CIP

This publication is made possible by generous gifts from the Daniel J. Boorstin Fund
and from Mr. and Mrs. Martin S. Davis.

Printed in the United States of America.

Designed by Gibson Design Associates.

Cover: Portrait of Thomas Jefferson by Charles Willson Peale, 1791. Courtesy Independence
National Historical Park.

The
DECLARATION
of
INDEPENDENCE

Thomas Jefferson, a medallion engraving by Saint-Mémin,
Washington, D.C., 1804. From the Prints and Photographs Division,
Library of Congress (LC–USZC4–5179)

Table of Contents ⋆

Preface

★ ★

HE STUDY OF THE EVOLUTION OF THE TEXT of the Declaration of Independence which the Library of Congress undertook while the nation was in the throes of World War II has remained for more than fifty years the preeminent textual presentation of the most fundamental document of the United States. In this publication the Library of Congress brought together for the first time photographic prints of all known drafts of the Declaration of Independence, publishing them in one large-format book with the cooperation and generous support of the American Philosophical Society, the Massachusetts Historical Society, and the New York Public Library.

The Library's presentation of Julian P. Boyd's textual analysis of the Declaration of Independence was part of a large wartime nationwide effort to celebrate America's fundamental freedoms in conjunction with the bicentennial of the birth of Thomas Jefferson, author of America's most basic document—the Declaration of Independence. The celebration was highlighted by the brief return of the engrossed, signed copy of the Declaration of Independence from its place of wartime safekeeping to Washington, D.C., for exhibition from April 12 to 19, 1943, at the newly opened Jefferson Memorial. There it was displayed for seven days under military guard before its return to Fort Knox, Kentucky. On October 1, 1944, the document was returned for good to Washington and was replaced in its specially designed shrine at the Library of Congress. In 1952 the engrossed copies of the Declaration of Independence and the U.S. Constitution were transferred from the Library of Congress to the National Archives by order of Congress's Joint Committee on the Library.

A moving wartime foreword by Archibald MacLeish, Librarian of Congress, and Julian Boyd's expert insights into the writing and editing of the text composed by Thomas Jefferson set the stage for this publication's presentation of the photographic reproductions. In it, readers could examine the documents, such as the Virginia Declaration of Rights, that Jefferson drew upon in preparing the Declaration of Independence. Moreover, readers could see that the writing of the Declaration was not an individual undertaking easily prepared, but rather that its composition involved diligent, determined cooperation in the midst of wartime chaos and danger, in which Jefferson had the zealous and constructive help of a committee of five delegates to Congress and indeed the involvement of the entire Continental Congress. Undoubtedly, the drafting of the text represented an example the authors hoped would not be lost on Americans in 1943.

The discovery in 1947 by Julian Boyd, Librarian at Princeton University and newly named documentary editor of *The Papers of Thomas Jefferson,* of a fragment of a previously unknown draft of the Declaration of Independence shed new light on earlier studies of its composition. This brief but critically important document fragment had been preserved unrecognized in the Thomas Jefferson Papers at the Library of Congress until Boyd's preparations for the new published edition of Jefferson's papers led him to reexamine these primary documents. The manuscript had been mistakenly filed under a September 1777 date with materials related to congressional consideration in 1776 of General John Sullivan's threatened resignation of his army commission after General Horatio Gates was appointed commander of the American army in Canada during its precipitous withdrawal to northern New York.

Heavily edited in Jefferson's own hand, the document proved to be a key component in unraveling the story of the writing of the Declaration of Independence. Boyd designated the document "the composition draft," to reflect its relevance to the composition of the text and to distinguish it from the fair copy labeled by Jefferson many years later as "Independence–Declaration original Rough draught." Boyd's carefully crafted study of the drafting of this fundamental testament needed reconsideration after his discovery of the fragment of the previously unknown composition draft. The existence of this fragment confirmed the view of those historians who had argued that a heavily edited draft must have preceded the most well-known and most revealing text of the Declaration of Independence, the copy Jefferson had endorsed as the original rough draft.

That the composition fragment was written before the "original Rough Draught" and then was corrected and copied into the "original Rough draught" was exactily explained by Boyd in 1950. "The Fragment contains several words and passages that are crossed out; none of these was copied into the 'Rough draught' (or true fair copy)," wrote Boyd in the explanatory note to the printing of the transcribed text of the draft fragment in the first volume of his edition of *The Papers of Thomas Jefferson*. "The Fragment also contains, in its undeleted 148 words that were copied in the 'Rough draught,' 43 words caretted and interlined; none of these was so treated in the 'Rough draught,'" according to Boyd.

Several additional and equally elaborate explanations were provided by Boyd in his textual note before he stated his opinion that "the most conclusive evidence" derived from Jefferson's writing the paragraph on the top of the half leaf of paper and leaving the remainder blank for subsequent corrections or drafts. The final two lines—"these facts have given the last stab to agonizing affection, & manly spirit bids us to renounce for ever these unjust unfeeling brethren" —were composed in this blank space before being interlined in the drafted paragraph. In late July 1776, Jefferson used the remainder of this blank half leaf to draft a resolution accepting the proffered resignation (received in Congress on July 26, 1776) of Continental Army general John Sullivan, who, insulted when General Gates was appointed commander of the American army in Canada on June 17, 1776, wished to resign his commission. Congress allowed Sullivan to withdraw this resignation and to continue to serve his country; later he was captured by the British at the time of their victory on Long Island.

Serious public and scholarly interest in the evolution of the text of the Declaration of Independence was renewed fifty years after Boyd's discovery when the Library of Congress first publicly exhibited the fragment of the composition draft in 1995. Both the fragment and the "original Rough draught" were made available by the Library of Congress on its home page on the Internet. Heightened public interest made it apparent that the rare copies of Library's 1943 publication or of the 1945 Princeton University Press edition that occasionally become available for public sale in the antiquarian book trade do not suffice to satisfy curiosity on this subject.

Thus the Library of Congress and the Thomas Jefferson Memorial Foundation, the private, nonprofit organization that owns and operates Monticello, decided to jointly reissue an updated edition of the 1943 Library of Congress publication. Through the generosity and dedication to scholarship of the American Philosophical Society, the Massachusetts Historical Society, the New York Public Library, and the National Archives and Records Administration, the latest technology has been used to produce the photographic reproductions in this volume. This preface, a photographic reproduction of the composition draft fragment with a brief explanatory note, and a few editorial insertions enclosed in angle brackets to make corrections or provide information have been the only textual additions to the new edition.

A generous grant from the Daniel J. Boorstin Fund, and the encouragement of Librarian of Congress Emeritus Daniel J. Boorstin and his wife and scholarly collaborator, Ruth Boorstin, have made this publication possible. In addition, Monticello received support for this project from Mr. and Mrs. Martin S. Davis.

Those seeking additional scholarly details of the writing of the Declaration of Independence should consult the following works: first and foremost, the work undertaken by Julian P. Boyd et al., editors, *The Papers of Thomas Jefferson,* 27 volumes to date (Princeton: Princeton University Press, 1950–), especially volume 1, pages 413–33; the Library's documentary edition *Letters of Delegates to Congress, 1774–1789,* 25 volumes (Washington: Library of Congress, 1976–), edited by Paul H. Smith et al., especially volume 4, pages 156–383; Julian P. Boyd's *The Declaration of Independence: The Evolution of the Text* (Princeton: Princeton University Press, 1945); a work by John H. Hazelton, *The Declaration of Independence: Its History* (New York: Dodd, Mead, and Company, 1906); and a related publication issued by the Library of Congress in 1976, *The John Dunlap Broadside: The First Printing of the Declaration of Independence* by Frederick Goff. Three important works for understanding the Declaration are Pauline Maier's *American Scripture: Making the Declaration of Independence* (New York: Knopf, 1997); *Inventing America: Jefferson's Declaration of Independence* by Garry Wills (Garden City, N.Y.: Doubleday, 1978); and Carl Becker's study, *The Declaration of Independence. A Study in the History of Political Ideas* (New York: Harcourt, Brace and Company, 1922).

Gerard W. Gawalt
Library of Congress

$$\star \quad \mathcal{F}oreword \quad \star$$

I N 1823 JEFFERSON SAID OF TIMOTHY PICKERING'S Fourth of July oration at Salem: "Timothy thinks … that the Declaration, as being a libel on the government of England, should now be buried in utter oblivion to spare the feelings of our English friends and Angloman fellow citizens. But it is not to wound them that we wish to keep it in mind; but to cherish the principles of the instrument in the bosoms of our own citizens.… I pray God that these principles may be eternal." The Library of Congress borrows Mr. Jefferson's phrase in publishing in the year 1943 this study of the text of the Declaration of Independence. It is not to wound our English friends and Angloman fellow citizens that we publish at this time a study of the evolution of the Declaration's text but to cherish the principles of the instrument in the bosoms of our own citizens.

The Declaration of Independence is a positive and not a negative document. It is less a declaration of independence from Great Britain than a declaration of independence for the United States: less an act of revolution against the tyranny of a mediocre and stubborn king than an act of revolution for a society of free, and freedom-loving, men.

To our enemies abroad it may seem paradoxical that the American people should celebrate, in the midst of a war which finds them fighting side by side with Englishmen, the birth and the achievement of the man who was the principal author of their independence from the British crown. To the British, however, and to ourselves, there is no paradox. The Declaration of Independence is one of the great precedents in the tradition of the liberty of English-speaking peoples and as such is a part of the British inheritance as it is of ours. Like the Magna Carta, which is now deposited among the treasures of the Library of Congress <where, in 1939, the Lincoln Cathedral copy had been placed for wartime safekeeping>, the Declaration of Independence has a common meaning to both peoples.

What was divisive in the Declaration—what set Americans against Englishmen and Englishmen against Americans—was its negative denunciation of the British rule. What is creative and unifying is its declaration of the basic principles of human liberty and its proposal for the future of a society in which human liberty could flourish. The negative aspects time has cancelled out. But never at any time in the history of either country was the affirmative and creative significance of the Declaration of Independence more living than it is today.

As men in the free countries of the world, beset by dangers from without and by doubts from within, grope for the meaning of their lives, they rediscover, with a new and sudden vividness of understanding, the hard and revolutionary realities of Jefferson's Declaration. For a century, and more than a century, the words Jefferson used had worn smooth in men's mouths.

The actual meaning had left them. They went from hand to hand like coins whose inscriptions all men recognize and no men read or see. But now in these dangerous years, when every pre-conception, every easy understanding, has been questioned by brutality and violence, the words take shape again and, taking shape, take meaning. Gradually out of the darkness of this time the image of the world which Jefferson imagined gathers the light and assumes the form it had to him and his contemporaries.

It is appropriate, therefore, and appropriate not to Americans only but to all those who respect the precedents of freedom, that the national library of the United States should publish in this year the various texts which illuminate the meaning of the Declaration of Independence. For the first time in the history of this country, the Library has brought together, in its <Thomas Jefferson> Bicentennial Exhibition, all but one of the known drafts and copies of the Declaration written by Jefferson. These drafts and copies, together with certain earlier American manuscripts from which the Declaration's principal ideas derive, have been pho-tographed and are here reproduced, as is also the single draft not included in the Library's Exhibit—that in the possession of the American Philosophical Society at Philadelphia. To these facsimiles—themselves eloquent to any discerning eye—has been added a commentary by Mr. Julian P. Boyd, the distinguished Librarian of Princeton University and the Historian of the Thomas Jefferson Bicentennial Commission.

An acknowledgment of the indebtedness of the Library of Congress to those who have contributed their labor and loaned their most valued possessions to its celebration of the Jefferson Bicentennial is expressed elsewhere. I cannot, however, close this brief Foreword without adding to the formal thanks of the Library of Congress my personal thanks on my own behalf and on behalf of my colleagues for the generous and self-sacrificing labor of Mr. Boyd and for the helpfulness, in a common enterprise of American scholarship, of the President and Board of Trustees of the New York Public Library, the President and Council of the Massa-chusetts Historical Society, the President and Council of the American Philosophical Society, the Officers of the Adams Manuscript Trust, and the Archivist of the United States and his colleagues.

Archibald MacLeish
THE LIBRARIAN OF CONGRESS

The Drafting of the Declaration of Independence

N A BROAD SENSE, THE AUTHOR of the Declaration of Independence was the American people.[1] Its great object was to formulate the principles of government in such a way as to justify rebellion, and the subject of government, as John Adams pointed out, was a subject discussed daily at almost every fireside in America on the eve of the Revolution. If, as Jefferson intended, the Declaration was "an expression of the American mind," he was in this sense the inspired amanuensis of the people. Like that other wide-ranging intellect of the eighteenth century, Benjamin Franklin, he was ever ready to acknowledge his derivative authorship, even when the felicity of his prose, the clarity of his expression, and the daring of his ideas combined to stamp the product of his pen as indubitably and singly Jeffersonian. Thus, as author of the far-reaching legal reforms in Virginia by which "every fibre would be eradicated of ancient or future aristocracy; and a foundation laid for a government truly republican," Jefferson, far from claiming sole authorship of this liberating system of laws, paid high tribute to his coadjutors George Mason and George Wythe.[2] Thus also did he respond to the busy efforts of a New England Federalist, Timothy Pickering, who early in the 19th century endeavored "to show how little was his merit in compiling" the Declaration.[3] What Pickering sought to prove was that Jefferson had contributed nothing original, nothing distinctively new, nothing solely Jeffersonian to the great apologia of the American Revolution. What he actually accomplished was to give Jefferson the opportunity to state the things that might have remained unspoken but for Pickering's gratuitous efforts.

The Fourth of July oration delivered at Salem by Pickering in 1823, almost two decades after he had set out to deprecate Jefferson's claim to authorship, quoted a letter from John Adams to the effect that the Declaration contained no idea "but what had been hackneyed in Congress for two years before."[4] Indeed, Adams had added, the substance of it was to be found in the Declaration of Rights of 1774 and "in a pamphlet, voted and printed by the town of Boston, before the first Congress met, composed by James Otis, as I suppose, in one of his lucid intervals, and pruned and polished by Samuel Adams." If by "the substance of it" Adams meant the nature and purpose of government, he was engaged in laboring the obvious, a forgivable trait in the aged statesman who had been called by Stockton of New Jersey "the Atlas of American Independence." But the obvious as uttered by Pickering and the obvious as stated by the venerable statesman of Braintree had two very distinct connotations. Adams may have been a trifle querulous, but Pickering was acting upon a definite purpose that he had stated so early as 1811. When he said that the Declaration contained only hackneyed ideas, he meant it as criticism, thereby exposing himself to the obvious response: the greatness of the Declaration lay in the very fact that it expressed what Adams himself had said was in the minds and hearts of the people.

Jefferson made such a response. "Pickering's observations, and Mr. Adams' in addition…" he wrote to Madison, "may all be true. Of that I am not to be the judge. Richard Henry Lee charged it as copied from Locke's treatise on Government…. I know only that I turned to neither book nor pamphlet while writing it. I did not consider it as any part of my charge to invent new ideas altogether and to offer no sentiment which had ever been expressed before." [5] The important task, as Jefferson further wrote May 8, 1825, to Henry Lee, was "Not to find out new principles, or new arguments, never before thought of, not merely to say things which had never been said before; but to place before mankind the common sense of the subject, [in] terms so plain and firm as to command their assent, and to justify ourselves in the independent stand we [were] impelled to take. Neither aiming at originality of principle or sentiment, nor yet copied from any particular and previous writing, it was intended to be an expression of the American mind…. All its authority rests then on the harmonizing sentiments of the day, whether expressed in conversation, in letters, printed essays, or the elementary books of public right, as Aristotle, Cicero, Locke, Sidney, etc." [6]

Thus did Jefferson share his authorship with the American people and thus did he identify the harmonizing sentiments of the day with concepts of government which had an ancient and diverse lineage. The idea that man was born equal, that he was possessed of certain inherent and unalienable rights, that these rights consisted of life, liberty, and the pursuit of happiness, that it was the duty of government to protect and preserve these rights, that the government which did not do so could be abolished—this was an idea familiar not only to those who had written "elementary books of public right," but also to every pamphleteer, every lawyer, every minister of the gospel, almost every American subject of George III in the epochal year 1776. Indeed, as one historian has put it, some of the American writers at the time of the Revolution "were acquainted with practically all of the exponents of the idea [of fundamental law] from Sophocles to Blackstone." [7] But John Locke, whose two treatises on government appeared in 1690, is generally accepted by historical and legal scholarship as the great fountainhead of Revolutionary thought in America. [8] He, too, like Jefferson, drew from many springs and was drawn from for many purposes. Even Thomas Hobbes, whose great *Leviathan* stood at the other pole from Locke, thought "all men are born equal, and by Nature Free," which, from an exponent of absolutism, was even more than Jefferson could put into the Declaration. The Revolutionary dialecticians employed ideas from whatever source bore authoritative weight, whether it was Aristotle or Cicero among the ancient writers; or Grotius, Pufendorf, Vattel, Burlamaqui, and Montesquieu among the Continentals; or Hooker, Hoadley, Locke, Sidney, and Buchanan in the great stream of English libertarian thought. [9] Jefferson himself, in the letter to Henry Lee in 1825, named some of the principal authors that he identified with the principles of the Declaration, and some significance has been attached to the fact that "Aristotle, Cicero, Locke, Sidney, etc." did not include the name of Montesquieu. Perhaps the date of this comment helps to explain the omission. But a recently published letter, dated in 1771, gives quite another emphasis and significance because it was written only five years before Jefferson penned the

Declaration. Robert Skipwith had asked the young Virginia lawyer to recommend a number of books "suited to the capacity of a common reader, who understands but little of the classics and has not leisure for any intricate or tedious study." The list that Jefferson drew up, impressive in range and character, included one category under the heading "Of Politics and Trade." On this head, Jefferson wrote, "I have given you a few only of the best books, as you would probably choose to be not unacquainted with those commercial principles which bring wealth into our country and the constitutional security we have for the enjoyment of that wealth."[10] The first item on the list was Montesquieu's *Spirit of Laws*. This was followed by Locke, Marmontel, Bolingbroke, and others. There can be no doubt, then, that five years before he drew up the Declaration, Jefferson regarded both Montesquieu and Locke as among the best authors of "elementary books of public right."

This is not to imply that Jefferson was guilty of plagiarizing the works of the classical authors on the subject of government. Some have seen similarity of phrase in the Declaration and in the second treatise by Locke; others have seen parallels between it and a passage in James Wilson's pamphlet, *Considerations on the Nature and Extent of the Legislative Authority of the British Parliament*. But even if Jefferson had "copied from any particular and previous writing," even if he had used an identifiable model—and his colleagues in Congress would have agreed as to the excellence of Locke—the most that would be proved by this is that he had failed to be original in an enterprise where originality would have been fatal. The greatness of his achievement, aside from the fact that he created one of the outstanding literary documents of the world and of all time, was that he identified its sublime purpose with the roots of liberal traditions that spread back to England, to Scotland, to Geneva, to Holland, to Germany, to Rome, and to Athens. In the fundamental statement of national purpose for a people who were to embrace many races and many creeds, nothing could have been more appropriate than that the act renouncing the ties of consanguinity should at the same time have drawn its philosophical justification from traditions common to all.

WHEN PAINE'S *COMMON SENSE* PROCLAIMED early in 1776 with the clear and rousing tones of a bugle that "the period of debate is over," the idea of independence grew with enormous rapidity. Even so late as June 1775 Jefferson had written to John Randolph: "I am sincerely one of those … who would rather be in dependence on Great Britain, properly limited, than on any other nation on earth, or than on no nation. But I am one of those, too, who, rather than submit to the rights of legislating for us, assumed by the British Parliament, and which late experience has shown they will so cruelly exercise, would lend my hand to sink the whole Island in the ocean." But by late spring of 1776 it was abundantly clear that reconciliation was not possible.

On May 15 two events occurred which effectively closed the door to all plans of accommodation between Great Britain and the American colonies. In the Virginia Convention at Williamsburg, just as Jefferson arrived in Philadelphia to take his seat in Congress, a resolution was adopted by which the Virginia delegates were instructed to "propose to that respectable body to declare the United Colonies free and independent States, absolved from all allegiance to, or dependence on, the Crown or Parliament of Great Britain; and that they give the assent of this Colony to such declaration, and to whatever measures may be thought proper and necessary by the Congress for forming foreign alliances, and a Confederation of the Colonies, at such time and in the manner as to them shall seem best: Provided, that the power of forming government for, and the regulations of the internal concerns of each Colony, be left to the respective Colonial legislatures." To this bold move there was only one dissenting voice in the Convention and on that day Williamsburg rejoiced as on a festive occasion: the troops were paraded, the artillery discharged, the town illuminated, and the Continental flag hoisted over the Capitol.[11] At the State House in Philadelphia, an event of equally solemn significance was taking place. A resolution, drafted by John Adams and recommending that the various colonies assume all the powers of government, was adopted. This was a move which Adams, as he later affirmed, "had invariably pursued for a whole year, and contended for, through a scene … of anxiety, labor, study, argument, and obloquy."[12] On May 17 he wrote to his wife: "Great Britain has at last driven America to the last step, a complete separation from her; a total absolute independence, not only of her Parliament but of her crown, for such is the amount of the resolve of the 15th. Confederation among ourselves, or alliances with foreign nations are not necessary to a perfect separation from Britain. That is effected by extinguishing all authority under the crown, Parliament, and nation, as the resolution for instituting governments has done, to all intents and purposes.… A whole government of our own choice, managed by persons whom we love, revere, and can confide in, has charms in it, for which men will fight.…"[13] James Duane of New York, one of the moderates from the Middle Colonies who did not share the radical feelings of his colleagues to the extreme North and South, told Adams that he thought this resolution "a machine for the fabrication of independence." Adams replied smilingly that he "thought it was independence itself, but we must have it with more formality yet."[14]

From May 15 onward the tide moving toward independence rose swiftly. On the 20th Elbridge Gerry expressed the opinion that the unbelievers were at last "convinced there is no medium between unqualified submission and actual Independency."[15] On May 27, as Congress discussed the ensuing military campaign with General Washington, the Virginia instructions concerning independence arrived, quickening the pace of events. On June 3, John Adams wrote to Patrick Henry that he thought the natural sequence of events was for every colony to institute its own government, for all the colonies to confederate and establish a constitution, for the confederated colonies then to declare themselves a sovereign state, or a number of confederated states; and, finally, for the confederation to form treaties with foreign powers. "But I fear we cannot proceed systematically," he added, "and that we shall be obliged to declare ourselves independent States, before we confederate, and indeed before all the colonies have established their governments. It is now pretty clear that all these measures will follow one another in a rapid succession, and it may not perhaps be of much importance which is done first."[16] On June 7 Richard Henry Lee—who, as John Adams expressed it, "agreed perfectly with us in our great system of policy"—put into effect the Virginia instructions by moving a resolution embodying all of the actions contemplated by Adams, save the one which Congress had already advanced. It was Adams who seconded the motion which, in the handwriting of Richard Henry

Lee, "Resolved, that these United Colonies are, and of right ought to be, free and independent States, that they are absolved from all allegiance to the British Crown, and that all political connection between them and the State of Great Britain is, and ought to be, totally dissolved."[17] Thus, after months of debate, was the great issue brought to the point of decisive action.

Congress postponed consideration of this motion until the next day, June 8, when the leaders of the moderates—James Wilson, Robert R. Livingston, John Dickinson, and Edward Rutledge—questioned the wisdom of declaring independence before the people of the Middle Colonies demanded it or alliances with foreign powers made it practicable to support such a move. Richard Henry Lee, John Adams, George Wythe and others opposed this view and, when Congress resumed the discussion on June 10, the moderates secured a postponement of three weeks. As Jefferson explained the situation in his *Notes,* "It appearing in the course of these debates that the colonies of N. York, New Jersey, Pennsylvania, Delaware, Maryland and South Carolina were not yet matured for falling from the parent stem, but that they were fast advancing to that state, it was thought most prudent to wait a while for them, and to postpone the final decision to July 1."[18] Since this postponement was carried by a vote of only seven states to five, and since the ultimate passage of Lee's Resolution of Independence was a foregone conclusion, it was thought prudent in the meantime to appoint a committee to draft a declaration. Thus, to carry out this purpose in the interval of the postponement, a committee composed of Thomas Jefferson, John Adams, Benjamin Franklin, Roger Sherman, and Robert R. Livingston was appointed on June 11. When Congress resumed discussion of the Lee Resolution of Independence on July 1, John Dickinson made another last effort to delay the impending decision, but John Adams, in a notable speech delivered at the particular request of the New Jersey delegates who had just arrived, recapitulated the long arguments of recent months and finally, on June 2 <July 2>, the political ties with England were severed by the adoption of the Lee Resolution of Independence.[19] This was the legal act of separation: what Jefferson and his committee had been engaged in the meantime in preparing was the formal announcement to the world proclaiming, as required by "a decent respect to the opinions of mankind," the reasons for the action that had been taken. It was this distinction that led John Adams to think that the real celebration of the anniversary would take place on July 2 rather than July 4. "The second day of July, 1776," he wrote to Abigail Adams, "will be the most memorable epocha in the history of America. I am apt to believe that it will be celebrated by succeeding generations as the great anniversary Festival. It ought to be commemorated, as the day of deliverance, by solemn acts of devotion to God Almighty. It ought to be solemnized with pomp and parade, with shows, games, sports, guns, bells, bonfires, and illuminations, from one end of this continent to the other, from this time forward, forevermore."[20]

In the same manner in which Locke's treatises had been written "to justify to the world the people of England, whose love of their just and natural rights, with their resolution to preserve them, saved the nation when it was on the very brink of slavery and ruin," the Declaration of Independence as prepared by Jefferson and adopted by Congress was not actually the vote of separation but was intended as "an appeal to the tribunal of the world ... for justification." As such, it bore no necessary antagonism to the idea of kingship in general but only postulated the theory that the right of revolution could be exercised when the particular form of government entered into by any people—whether monarchy, aristocracy, or republic—violated the trust committed to it.[21] Grounded upon this postulate was the sonorous indictment of George III, its long catalogue of injustices implying not so much the wrongness of the deeds as the sinister malignancy of the royal will that prompted the doing of them. The task assigned to Jefferson was to act as advocate of his country's cause before the bar of world opinion.

IN THE PREFACE TO THE SECOND EDITION of his brilliant book entitled *The Declaration of Independence: a Study in the History of Political Ideals,* Mr. Carl Becker inferentially apologizes for including fifty-nine pages of textual criticism of the various preliminary drafts of the Declaration as being "mostly irrelevant to the main theme." Thomas Jefferson thought otherwise. In his *Notes* he indicated the text of the Declaration "as originally reported" and as excised by Congress. In doing this he may have been moved by the natural pride of an author in so great a document, but his expressed reason was that "the sentiments of men are known not only by what they receive, but what they reject also."[22] Mr. Becker's analysis of the textual evolution of the Declaration is so clearly and painstakingly presented that there is no valid ground for doubt that, on this point, he and Jefferson are in perfect accord. The following pages, bringing together for the first time facsimiles of all of the drafts made by Jefferson that are known to be extant, will attempt in summary form to present most of the significant changes that took place in the text from the time that Jefferson presented it to his colleagues on the Committee of Five to the time that Congress adopted it as amended on July 4. It should become obvious in the course of this analysis that the sentiments of Congress were indicated both by what they rejected from the draft and by what they added to it.

Jefferson, except for Robert R. Livingston, was the youngest member of the Committee of Five and he had taken his seat in Congress only one day before the decisive resolution of May 15. John Adams, on the other hand, had labored during the whole winter, pressing hard for independence. In the course of time the question naturally arose as to why young Jefferson—he was then thirty-three—was given the post of honor on this most important of all committees. "There were more reasons than one," John Adams answered: "Mr. Jefferson came into Congress in June 1775, and brought with him a reputation for literature, science, and a happy talent of composition. Writings of his were handed about remarkable for the peculiar felicity of expression. Though a silent member in Congress, he was so prompt, frank, explicit and decisive upon committees and in conversation … that he soon seized upon my heart, and upon this occasion I gave him my vote and did all in my power to procure the votes of others. I think he had one more vote than any other, and that placed him at the head of the Committee. I had the next highest number and that placed me second."[23]

Jefferson's writing of the original draft of the Declaration and his consultations with members of the Committee of Five took place in the seventeen days between the appointment of the Committee on June 11 and its report of the draft to Congress on June 28. During this interval Jefferson was living in the new brick home of a young German by the name of Graaf or Graff on the southwest corner of Market and Seventh streets. In the parlor of the second floor, across the hall from his bedroom, Jefferson "wrote habitually and … this paper [the Declaration] particularly."[24] There appears to be no contemporary evidence to show the procedure by which the Committee of Five selected Jefferson to prepare a preliminary draft, and the account given by John Adams in 1805 and again in 1822 is, unhappily, different from that given by Jefferson in 1823. In his *Autobiography*, Adams gave the following account of the drafting: "The Committee had several Meetings, in which were proposed the articles of which the Declaration was to consist, and minutes made of them. The Committee then appointed Mr. Jefferson and me, to draw them up in form, and cloath them in proper Dress. The Sub Committee met, and considered the Minutes, making such Observations on them as then occurred: when Mr. Jefferson desired me to take them to my lodgings and make the Draught. This I declined and gave several reasons for declining (1) that he was a Virginian and I a Massachusettensian. (2) that he was a Southern Man and I a northern one. (3) that I had been so obnoxious for my early and constant Zeal in promoting the Measure, that any draught of mine, would undergo a more severe Scrutiny and Criticism in Congress, than one of his composition. 4thly and lastly, and that would be reason enough if there were no other, I had a great opinion of the Elegance of his pen, and none at all of my own. I there-fore insisted that no hesitation should be made on his part. He accordingly took the Minutes and in a day or two produced to me his Draught. Whether I made or suggested any corrections I remember not. The Report was made to the Committee of five, by them examined, but whether altered or corrected in any thing I cannot recollect. But in Substance at least it was reported to Congress where, after a Severe Criticism, and Striking out several of the most oratorical Paragraphs it was adopted on the fourth of July 1776, and published to the World."[25] In his letter of 1822 to Timothy Pickering, Adams gave a similar account of the drafting, adding that "We were all in haste; Congress was impatient and the Instrument was reported, I believe in Jefferson's hand writing as he first drew it."[26] When this letter came to Jefferson's attention, he wrote to Madison giving the following version: "Mr. Adams's memory has led him into unquestionable error…. The Committee of 5 met, no such thing as a subcommittee was proposed, but they unanimously pressed on myself alone to undertake the draught. I consented; I drew it; but before I reported it to the committee, I communicated it separately to Dr. Franklin and Mr. Adams requesting their corrections; because they were the two members of whose judgments and amendments I wished most to have the benefit before presenting it to the Committee; and you have seen the original paper[27] now in my hands, with the corrections of Doctor Franklin and Mr. Adams interlined in their own handwritings. Their alterations were two or three only, and merely verbal. I then wrote a fair copy,[28] reported it to the Committee, and from them, unaltered to Congress. This personal communication and consultation with Mr. Adams he has misremembered into the meetings of a subcommittee."[29] Jefferson said that his own version was "supported by written notes, taken by myself at the moment and on the spot," but these notes leave much to be desired in the way of information. They merely say that "The Committee for drawing the declaration of Independence desired me to do it. It was accordingly done, and being approved by them, I reported it to the House on Friday, the 28th of June, when it was read, and ordered to lie on the table."[30]

In the efforts of historians to reconcile the statements of Adams and Jefferson, attention has been focussed so much upon the chief point of contradiction—whether there was a subcommittee or not—that other parts of Adams' statement that went unchallenged by Jefferson have been overlooked. It may be <of> some significance, for example, that Jefferson does not deny that the Committee "discussed the subject." Adams, in the similar statement in <his> *Autobiography,* is more explicit on this point: "The Committee had several Meetings, in which were proposed the articles of which the Declaration was to consist and minutes made of them." Jefferson, in all probability, never saw this more extended statement, but the fact remains that he did not challenge, in the document that he did see, the statement that there was a discussion of the subject. Even conceding the question of unanimity in the Committee as to the desire to have Jefferson write the Declaration, it is quite unlikely that there was no discussion of the form the Declaration was to take. The probability is that no formal minutes were taken, as Adams suggests, but it is possible that the Committee acted on this occasion as a similar committee did in the Federal Convention eleven years later, by separating the subject into various headings and directing Jefferson to put the Declaration in proper form.[31] His primary object, of course, was to explain and justify the adoption by Congress of the Lee Resolution of Independence, and it is hardly conceivable that a committee including such astute men as Adams, Sherman, Franklin, and Livingston would not have canvassed the arguments by which this was to be done. Those arguments, to be sure, had been "hackneyed in Congress" for some time past, but in all probability there must have been some discussion in the Committee as to the codification, arrangement, amplification, and emphasis to be given.

When Jefferson sat down to his task in the parlor of the young German bricklayer, he "turned to neither book nor pamphlet while writing" the Declaration, according to the statement he made to Madison in 1823. Nor, as he said in the same letter, did he copy it "from any particular and previous writing." This, of course, may be symbolically true, even for a document which was supposed to be "an expression of the American mind" and therefore to be drawn from every source giving access to public and private thinking on the great issue. Yet it is scarcely possible that Jefferson could have escaped a conscious or unconscious reliance on two notable Virginia documents of the preceding weeks, one of which he wrote and the other of which he knew as thoroughly as he knew his Locke from which in large measure it came. The former was his own draft of a proposed constitution for Virginia, a part of which was adopted on June 29, 1776, as the Preamble to the Virginia Constitution and the latter was George Mason's "Declaration of Rights … recommended to posterity as the Basis and Foundation of their Government," the famous Bill of Rights of Virginia which was adopted by the Convention of that State on June 12, 1776.

Jefferson's original draft of a fundamental law for his native State is a six-page folio document endorsed in his handwriting as follows: "Constitution of Virginia first ideas of Th: J. communicated to a member of the Convention."[32] This document was prepared by Jefferson sometime during the spring of 1776, perhaps after May 27 when the Virginia resolutions of May 15 were laid before Congress and certainly before June 13, 1776, when George Wythe—by whose hand it was sent to Edmund Pendleton, President of the Virginia Convention—departed for

Williamsburg. Three copies of this document, all in Jefferson's handwriting, are extant, two in the Library of Congress and one in the New York Public Library. The latter and the draft endorsed "first ideas" contain a catalogue of sixteen charges calculated to show how George III, "heretofore entrusted with the exercise of the kingly office in this government, hath endeavored to pervert the same into a detestable and insupportable tyranny." Jefferson, who must have kept at least one of the rough copies of this document by him in Philadelphia—perhaps the one here reproduced as Document II, since it is yet to be found in the Jefferson papers—could scarcely have avoided being influenced by it and indeed he did actually use it for his similar and some-what longer indictment of George III in the Declaration. His ideas on the Virginia Constitution arrived too late to be incorporated in that document, but the catalogue of royal misdeeds was adopted as the Preamble to the Constitution, followed immediately by George Mason's Bill of Rights. After this had been done, Edmund Pendleton, having seen both this document and the Declaration of Independence, wrote to Jefferson on July 22: "I expected you had in the Preamble to our form of Government, exhausted the Subject of Complaint against George 3d & was at a loss to discover what the Congress would do for one to their Declaration of Independence with-out copying but I find you have acquitted yourselves very well on that score."[33] It is not to be wondered at that Jefferson should have remembered and copied a document so recent and so fresh in his mind—a document, indeed, which had an identical purpose with that upon which he was now engaged: for, as he himself explained in 1825 in a letter to Judge Augustus B. Woodward, "The fact is that that preamble was prior in composition to the Declaration, and both having the same object, of justifying our separation from Great Britain, they used neces-sarily the same materials of justification: and hence their similitude."[34]

Indeed, such a justification in such a manner was likewise made in July, 1775, when Jefferson drew up the "Declaration ... setting forth the causes and necessity of ... taking up arms." But in that list of British injustices there was this great difference: the malignant will aimed at was not that of the King but of Parliament. The Declaration of Causes for taking up arms used the plural instead of the singular pronoun—"*They* have cut off the commercial inter-course of whole colonies with foreign countries; *they* have extended the jurisdiction of courts of admiralty beyond their ancient limits; *they* have deprived us of the inestimable privilege of trial by a jury of the vicinage," etc., etc.[35] The substance was the same, but implicit in this change of the pronoun between July, 1775, and July, 1776, was the American conception of the constitution of the British Empire around which the whole issue centered—a theory stated superbly well by Jefferson in his *Summary View of the Rights of British America* in 1774 and heralding in the American Revolutionary period what at last became a full reality in the imperial constitution of Great Britain in the adoption of the Statute of Westminster in 1931: that the colonies were virtually self-governing dominions and united in the Empire only by their common allegiance to the King and not, therefore, subject to Parliament.

For this reason—that Jefferson had been stating and restating the justification for the American position for so many months—it is not surprising that such exact parallels can be found between the Preamble to the Virginia Constitution and the draft of the Declaration of Independence as to indicate that he had before him and copied, in large part verbatim, the draft of the earlier document. In the first place, the sequence of the charges against the Crown in the Preamble is, with two exceptions, precisely that of the similar accusations in the Declaration. Next, the phraseology in both documents is so exactly parallel as to require only one example to prove a copied rather than a remembered process of composition: in the Preamble Jefferson wrote that the King had perverted his office "by denying to his governors permission to pass laws of immediate & pressing importance, unless suspended in their operation for his assent, &, when so suspended, neglecting to attend to them for many years." In the Declaration this weakly negative way of stating the charge—a style which was followed throughout the Preamble—was put with far greater force and dignity: "He has forbidden his Governors to pass Laws of immediate and pressing Importance, unless suspended in their Operation, till his Assent should be obtained; and when so suspended he has neglected utterly to attend to them."[36] "Neglected utterly" may have been more distant from historical truth—Jefferson, it should be remembered, was on this occasion an advocate and not an historian—than "neglected … for many years," but it was certainly more forceful and more appropriate to the occasion.

The other Virginia document that has generally been accorded a primary influence in the drafting of the Declaration is George Mason's Declaration of Rights, which Jefferson saw in the *Pennsylvania Evening Post* for June 6.[37] But in this case there is no such parallel in the sequence of clauses and little or none in identity of phrase as between the two documents. The similarity that exists is a similarity of ideas: Jefferson and Mason were both dealing with the concept of natural, inherent rights and on this subject both appealed, as all men of the day did, to Locke and other exponents of the idea of the social compact, the inviolability of rights, the trusteeship nature of government, and the right of revolution. The first and other paragraphs of Mason's Declaration of Rights have been quoted by respectable authorities as proof of Jefferson's dependence upon his fellow Virginian for that part of his Declaration dealing with broad theories of government. As given in Document I of this publication, Mason's first paragraph reads: "That all men are born equally free and independant and have certain inherent natural Rights, of which they can not, by any Compact, deprive or divest their Posterity; among which are the Enjoyment of Life and Liberty, with the Means of Acquiring and possessing property, and pursuing and obtaining Happiness and Safety." The Declaration of Rights goes on to state the axiomatic concepts of government that prevailed: sovereign power rested in the people; officials of government existed for the common benefit and security; and when any government was found unworthy of its trust, a majority of the community "hath an indubitable, inalienable and indefe[n]sible Right to reform, alter or abolish it.…" Even Jefferson did not state the right of revolution more emphatically, though he did it more simply and more effectively. The fact is that these broad concepts, familiar to any reader of Locke or Burlamaqui or Vattel, were so much a part of the air breathed by the patriots of 1776 that Jefferson could not have escaped using them and their more or less fixed phraseology even if he had desired to do so. It is very doubtful whether any idea or phrase used by Mason could not be found in the controversial literature of the day.

This is not to say that Jefferson was unimpressed by Mason's stirring Declaration of Rights: it appealed to the mind and spirit of the whole Continent. Yet, with the armory of argument not only furnished but imposed upon him by the logic of circumstances, what remained was for him to organize his materials in his own way and to express them in his own exalted and felicitous phraseology. At this sort of task he was a recognized master, not an unimaginative imitator, and he had been chosen for the great duty largely because of this known mastery of language: only one other genius of prose sat in the Congress—Benjamin Franklin— and wise, graceful, and witty though his writings were, Franklin was not given to reaching such majestic heights as was Jefferson's habit. That Jefferson was influenced by and copied his own words in his proposed constitution for Virginia is inescapably proved by a cursory comparison of that document with the Declaration. That he was as directly influenced by the Mason Declaration is not yet proved and must in all probability remain a matter of opinion.

THE VARIOUS TEXTS OF THE DECLARATION in Jefferson's handwriting that are known to be extant are six <in 1943, now seven> in number, one <or, two of the seven> of them fragmentary. These, together with the highly important copy taken by and in the handwriting of John Adams, provide the materials for tracing the evolution of the text through its formative history. Four decades ago Paul Leicester Ford described all of these known drafts. In the time that has elapsed since that date—though Jefferson is known to have sent copies between July 4 and 10 to John Page, Edmund Pendleton, George Wythe, and Philip Mazzei, in addition to that known as the Richard Henry Lee copy—no other complete drafts have come to light. These texts in the handwriting of Jefferson are as follows: (1) the Rough Draft which was endorsed by Jefferson "original Rough draft" (reproduced here as Document V); (2) the copy made for Richard Henry Lee (reproduced as Document VI); (3) the copy in the Emmet Collection of the New York Public Library, sent to an unidentified person and referred to here as the Cassius F. Lee copy (reproduced as Document VII); (4) the copy made by Jefferson for James Madison in 1783 from the draft in the *Notes* which Jefferson made in Congress during the debates on the Declaration (reproduced as Document VIII); (5) the draft in the *Notes* from which the Madison copy was taken; and (6) the incomplete copy in the Washburn Papers of the Massachusetts Historical Society (referred to as the Washburn copy and reproduced as Document IX); <and (7), discovered in 1947, the composition document fragment, reproduced here as Document IIIA>. In any study of these Jefferson drafts and copies, four other texts must be taken into consideration: the copy taken by John Adams (reproduced here as Document IV) and the three official texts. The first of the official texts is the John Dunlap broadside which was probably printed the night of July 4–5 and then wafered into the Rough Journal of Congress, in which a blank space had been left for it, reproduced here as Document X. The second is the copy in the Corrected Journal of Congress which is written out by hand rather than printed and the third is the engrossed parchment copy which was signed by the delegates. It would be supposed that the Corrected Journal of Congress would, in all likelihood, be the most authoritative official text, but the Corrected Journal omits two words that are to be found in the copy in the Rough Journal and in all other texts, including the engrossed copy.[38] Even in the official texts capitalization and punctuation are, to understate the case, not uniform and are disregarded in all of the comparative remarks in these pages. For, as Mr. Becker has so engagingly put it in referring to the engrossed copy:

"The capitalization and punctuation, following neither previous copies, nor reason, nor the custom of any age known to man, is one of the irremediable evils of life to be accepted with becoming resignation." This we may lay at the feet of the man who engrossed the great document, remembering as we do so that an unknown compositor in the printing plant of John Dunlap, working through the night of July 4, preserved for us what remains today the first official and perhaps the most authoritative text.

Inasmuch as Jefferson's Rough Draft was submitted to Adams twice and perhaps also to Franklin, there are three distinct stages that must be considered in the evolution of the Declaration: (1) as it was when Jefferson presented it to Franklin and Adams in advance of a meeting with the Committee and secured Adams' and perhaps Franklin's corrections; (2) as it was when reported by the Committee of Five to Congress; and (3) as it was when Congress had completed its additions and deletions. It would be impossible to arrive at even an approximation of these stages if it were not for the fact that the Rough Draft stands flanked by the Adams and other copies. The Adams copy gives an approximation of the text in its earlier stages and the Madison, Richard Henry Lee, and other copies indicate changes that occurred in the final phase. Using these copies in his textual analysis, Mr. Becker was able to arrive at the text of the Declaration as it stood at various points in its progress. He presented this text by the always difficult and frequently impossible method of representing unconfined script through the medium of inflexible type, whereas with the use of facsimiles a different approach is possible. Though the result in one sense will appear disconnected it will in another sense be clarified by the opportunity to refer to photographic reproductions. The approach to be used here is to consider the Rough Draft as the surveyor's bench mark, as it were, and the Adams and Lee copies as triangulation points, from which, by a series of additions and subtractions of changes that were made at various stages, some approximation of the text may be arrived at though the text itself will not be given in full. The problem is enormously complicated by the fact that changes in the text consisted of both deletions and additions, to say nothing of the fact that no one can tell precisely where our two triangulation points are located: even the bench mark shifts occasionally, for Jefferson himself made alterations in the text, it may be assumed, at almost every stage in its progress.

There can scarcely be any question but that the Rough Draft is the most extraordinarily interesting document in American history. Neither the manuscripts of the various plans of government submitted to the Federal Convention of 1787 nor James Wilson's original manuscript of the Federal Constitution can quite compare with it. For it embodies in its text and in its multiplicity of corrections, additions, and deletions all, or almost all, of the Declaration as it was at every stage of its journey from its origin in the parlor of Graff's home to its emergence in full glory as the authenticated and official charter of liberty of the American people. It thus contains within itself almost the whole story of the evolution of the Declaration, but that evolution became so hopelessly telescoped that even Jefferson himself was not, in later years, altogether clear as to the time at which some changes took place. "How then," asks Mr. Becker, "can we reconstruct the text of the Declaration as it read when Jefferson first submitted it to Franklin and Adams? For example, Jefferson first wrote 'We hold these truths to be sacred &

undeniable.' In the Rough Draft as it now reads, the words 'sacred & undeniable' are crossed out, and 'self-evident' is written in above the line. Was this correction made by Jefferson in process of composition? Or by the Committee of Five? Or by Congress? There is nothing in the Rough Draft itself to tell us."[39] Fortunately, the Adams copy was made at an early stage of the Rough Draft, for, as calculated here,[40] only fifteen of an ultimate total of eighty-six alterations had been made when Adams transcribed it, and these were chiefly of a minor character. One of these had certainly been made by Adams himself, possibly one or even two by Franklin, and the remainder by Jefferson. If we take these alterations into account by a comparison of the Adams copy with the Rough Draft, it will be possible to arrive approximately at the basic text of the Rough Draft as it stood when Jefferson presented it to what Adams called a subcommittee and what Jefferson, cleaving a fine hair, called a preliminary consultation. If the Rough Draft as reproduced here could be imagined with not more than fifteen short alterations, it would seem clear that, as will be suggested later, it was a fair copy of an earlier draft or notes for a draft.

The changes that had been made in the text of the Rough Draft as it was when Adams copied it are as follows:

Page One of the Rough Draft: (1) line 7,[41] "sacred & undeniable" changed to "self-evident." This famous and altogether felicitous change has been attributed both to Adams and to Jefferson. Such feeling as it exhibits for precisely the right word is quite Franklinian in character, but the handwriting in the phrase "self-evident" bears the appearance of being equally Jeffersonian. I find it difficult to believe that the characteristically Jeffersonian "s" here—another example appears immediately above it—and the even more distinctive final "t" with its peculiar "A"-like quality, were not made by Jefferson. The matter, however, must rest at present upon the amateur's feeling for distinctions, rather than upon any scientific analyses. Fitzpatrick thought that Franklin unquestionably wrote "self-evident"; Mr. Becker was undecided but thought the handwriting resembled Franklin's, as perhaps it does. But this divergence of views must be considered in connection with alteration (4) below, a change which has puzzled many; (2) line 9, "in" deleted before "rights"; (3) line 22, "subject" changed to "reduce"; (4) line 23, "to arbitrary" changed to "under absolute." At first glance it appears as if the words "to arbitrary power" were cancelled by two parallel lines with two continuous strokes of the pen and as if "Despotism" was written above this cancellation at the same time as "under absolute." Strangely, however, Adams did not copy the phrase as "under absolute Despotism" but as "under absolute power." This, as Mr. Becker observes, "is neither the original nor the corrected reading, but a combination of both. Adams may of course have made a mistake in copying (he made a number of slight errors in copying); or it may be that at this time Franklin wrote in 'under absolute' in place of 'to arbitrary' and that not until later, after Adams had made his copy, was 'power' crossed out and 'Despotism' written in. In the original manuscript, 'Despotism' appears to have been written with a different pen, or with heavier ink, than 'under Absolute,' as if written at a different time."[42] I think Mr. Becker is quite right in suggesting that "under absolute" and "Despotism" were written at different times and the latter after Adams had taken his copy. Both Adams' copying and the differences in shading in the words point to this conclusion. But I would go much further than Mr. Becker, though not without some trepidation. I would suggest that "under absolute" and "Despotism" were written at different times—and by different persons, the former by Jefferson before Adams took his copy and the latter by Franklin after Adams had done so. The three words "under absolute Despotism" have always been attributed to Franklin because of Jefferson's marginal notation opposite them, "Dr. Franklin's handwriting," with an identifying mark before each phrase connecting them with one another. It seems clear, however, that Jefferson's marginal notations were written many years after 1776, as the feebleness of the handwriting indicates; it is apparent also that Jefferson failed in these marginalia to give Franklin credit for all of the changes that were made by him in the Rough Draft. Could he have been mistaken in this instance likewise in giving Franklin credit for too much? It appears plausible in the light of the Adams copy and almost conclusive in the light of the differences in writing that "under absolute" and "Despotism" were not only written at different times but by different persons: the "s" in "absolute" appears markedly different from those in "Despotism"; the "u" certainly has a Jeffersonian appearance; the "t's" in the two words are different or appear to be; there is, as Mr. Becker points out, the striking difference in the shading of the words; the word "absolute" bears a very strong resemblance to the same word in the third line from the bottom of the same page; and finally, the strokes of the pen by which the phrase "to arbitrary power" is cancelled out were not continuous, as will be seen when the lines are examined under a powerful magnifying glass. Indeed, it is possible to see even in the accompanying reproduction the beginning of the lower line which crossed out "power" : its beginning occurs below and a hair's-breadth to the left of the "y" in "arbitrary," not quite touching the base of the "r" and not quite coinciding with the end of the lower of the two lines which crossed out "to arbitrary." This is indeed drawing the point rather fine, but upon this—taken in connection with the evidence of Adams' copying of the phrase—depends in some measure a possible solution of the question as to whether Jefferson presented the Declaration first to Adams instead of to Franklin as is generally supposed.

If my interpretation of these alterations is correct, both as to "self-evident" and "under absolute," then it appears that Franklin had made no changes in the text when Adams made his copy of the Rough Draft. This would indicate that Jefferson presented the Rough Draft to Adams first, who then made his copy, and later to Franklin. Such an interpretation is quite plausible in the light of a letter written by Franklin to George Washington on June 21: "I am just recovering a severe fit of the Gout, which has kept me from Congress and Company almost ever since you left us, so that I know little of what has pass'd there, except that a Declaration of Independence is preparing.…"[43] This was ten days after the Committee had been charged with its responsibility. We may suppose that Jefferson, finding Franklin ill and confined to his home, presented his Rough Draft to Adams first and Adams then made his copy.[44] If it is correct to assume that Jefferson, rather than Franklin, is really responsible for the alterations involving "self-evident" and "under absolute," then it appears that Adams, before he took his copy, had made only one change and Jefferson himself had made the others in process of composition, all of them before Adams copied the Rough Draft.

Page Two of the Rough Draft: (5) line 7, "in the legislature" inserted after "representation"; (6) line 8 "[illegible]" erased and "only" written over it; (7) line 11, "he has dissolved" struck out;

(8) line 11, "long space of time" changed by Adams to read in Rough Draft "long time after such Dissolutions" but Adams restored "space of" before "time" in his copy.

Page Three of the Rough Draft: (9) line 14, "subjects" erased and "citizens" written over it; (10) lines 21–22, "determined to keep open a market where MEN should be bought & sold" bracketed here for deletion and "determining to keep open a market where MEN should be bought & sold" inserted instead after "commerce" in line 24. The Committee—or Jefferson— later restored the original wording and sequence. (11) line 31, "y" in "injury" erased and word changed to "injuries"; (12) line 34, "12" erased and "twelve" written over it.

Page Four of the Rough Draft: (13) line 23, "glory &" deleted before, and "& to glory" insert- ed after, "happiness"; (14) lines 23–24, "in a separately state" deleted and "apart from them" inserted; (15) line 24, "pronounces" changed to "denounces"; (16) line 25, "everlasting Adieu!" deleted and "eternal separation" added.

Yet all this leaves several questions unanswered, the most important of which has been raised before: was this Rough Draft, incorporating only a few brief alterations, the first state of the document? Were there others that preceded it? If not, then the manuscript that Jefferson handed to Adams had presented far less difficulty in composition than his "first ideas" on the Virginia Constitution or his Declaration of Causes for Taking up Arms. When Jefferson wrote to Madison in 1823 saying "you have seen the original paper now in my hands, with the correc- tions of Dr. Franklin and Mr. Adams interlined in their own handwriting," he was undoubtedly referring to the Rough Draft. But did he intend to imply by the words "original paper" that there were no other drafts preceding it? If there were such copies drawn up in the process of compo- sition, why, it may be asked, are they not also in the Jefferson papers along with the Rough Draft? A fair question, but in view of the history of the Jefferson manuscripts, the absence of any other "original" draft or notes does not prove that such were not made: until recent years the three manuscript copies of Jefferson's drafts of a constitution for Virginia were to be found in three different places. It is not very likely that even Jefferson could have produced at the first attempt such a state paper as the Declaration with so few corrections, additions, and interlin- eations as the Rough Draft had when he showed it to Adams. On this point we do not have to rely altogether upon assumptions. There is evidence in the Rough Draft itself, the significance of which apparently has been hitherto overlooked, pointing to the fact that the Rough Draft was copied by Jefferson from another and earlier document or documents. On page two of the Rough Draft, Jefferson wrote these words (which are now almost obliterated but which we can reconstruct with the aid of the Adams copy): "he has dissolved Representative houses repeated- ly & continually for opposing with manly firmness his invasions on the rights of the people." Immediately following this paragraph, Jefferson wrote "he has dissolved" again, when, realizing that he had repeated himself, he drew a line through the words and proceeded firmly with the next paragraph. The remainder of the paragraph does not bear the appearance of an author groping for words.[45] The paragraph in which this repetition occurred is one of the most involved and difficult in the entire list of charges against George III, but, having made a false start, Jefferson proceeds smoothly and unhesitatingly to express a complicated idea or ideas, in extremely clear language, without another false move.[46] It appears obvious that the false start in this paragraph was made because Jefferson was copying from another document. Certainly the weight of evidence seems to bear out this interpretation and to invalidate the other. Moreover, we have evidence, in a remarkable coincidence, that Jefferson made precisely the same error in precisely the same paragraph when he was admittedly engaged in copying. This was in 1783 when, in copying the Declaration for Madison from the *Notes* that he had made of the debates in Congress, he committed the typical copyist's error of repeating the words "he has dissolved representative houses repeatedly …" and then struck out the repetition.[47] In short, the weight of evidence seems to point to the fact that in making the Rough Draft as it was when he presented it to Adams, Jefferson was copying from an earlier draft, and no doubt he did this in order to present a fair copy to Adams and Franklin.[48] Even so, he found it necessary or desirable to make several alterations as he went along.

Before proceeding to the next stage of evolution of the Declaration, one other question pertinent to the Rough Draft in all of its phases should be raised. How can we be certain that Adams and Franklin did not suggest some of the corrections that appeared in Jefferson's handwriting? How can we be certain whether some of these corrections and changes that took place between the time Jefferson drafted it and June 28 were not suggested by Adams or Franklin— or even by Roger Sherman, a very wise man, or by Robert R. Livingston, an intelligent youngster? Is it not likely that Jefferson took down in his own handwriting the corrections and changes as suggested by others and entered them in the Rough Draft, just as he did in Congress when his work was altered by that body?[49] The correct answer to these questions may be the one that Jefferson himself gave to Madison in 1823 that, after obtaining the "two or three" verbal alterations from Franklin and Adams, he then "wrote a fair copy, reported it to the committee, and from them unaltered to the Congress."[50] Mr. Becker thinks that Jefferson "was probably right in the assertion that no changes were made in the Committee." There appears to be no known documentary evidence to prove Jefferson wrong in the statement made to Madison. It is reasonable to assume that, having a majority of the Committee in consultation and in agreement with him, Jefferson would feel that he could make a fair copy with some hope of having it passed by Sherman and Livingston without drastic alteration.[51] It is probable too that Jefferson consulted Adams and Franklin more than once and perhaps several times; we know that he submitted the Rough Draft to Adams at least twice. We know, too, that subsequent to the making of the Adams copy a large number of changes took place in the Rough Draft. These were not merely verbal changes in every instance, for Jefferson added three whole paragraphs in his own hand. If Jefferson was in reality the author of all, or almost all, of the changes made in his handwriting and if Adams and Franklin added their changes before a fair copy was made for the formal approval of the Committee, then Jefferson could have been technically correct in his assertion that the fair copy passed the Committee without alteration. But this must remain, plausible though it may be, merely an assumption, somewhat shaken by the point made by Mr. Becker that one of the three paragraphs added in Jefferson's hand (the one embodied on the slip of paper pasted by Jefferson on page two of the Rough Draft) bears evidence of being the sort of change that Adams very likely might have suggested.

BUT, TO PROCEED TO THE SECOND STAGE, how can it be ascertained what changes were made before the Committee approved the Declaration and reported it to Congress? These numerous changes that appear in the Rough Draft, made singly or collectively by the Committee of Five—how do we know which were made by the Committee and which were made by Congress in the spirited debates on July 2 to 4? The fair copy asserted by Jefferson to have passed the Committee unaltered would have answered this question, but that fair copy is not known to be in existence. The Rough <Draft> copy, in itself, cannot tell us, for it is a maze of corrections made at all stages of the evolution of the text. Fortunately, we have workable substitutes for the missing fair copy in the Madison copy, in the Richard Henry Lee copy, in the copy in the *Notes* compiled by Jefferson between July 4, 1776, and June 1, 1783, from which the Madison copy was made, and in the Cassius F. Lee copy. By using these copies in comparison with the Rough Draft as it stood after Adams had made his copy, it is possible to arrive at the number of changes made before the Declaration went to Congress. This can be done owing to the fact that these copies, in one way or another—usually by underscoring, bracketing, or marginal notations—isolate the alterations attributable to Congress. Thus this identification of changes made in Congress was indicated in the copy sent to Madison by having "the parts struck out … distinguished by a black line drawn under them; & those inserted … placed in the margin or in a concurrent column." [52] The same thing is indicated in the Lee copy, the copy in Jefferson's *Notes,* and the Cassius F. Lee copy in similar but varying ways. Thus by comparing these copies with the Rough Draft and by excluding the corrections made in Congress, we shall arrive at the total number of changes made by Jefferson or by the Committee in the second phase of the evolution of the text.

The following are approximately the changes thus made in the second stage:

Page One of the Rough Draft: (1) line 1, "a" changed to "one"; (2) line 2, "advance from that subordination in which they have hitherto remained, & to" struck out and changed to "dissolve the political bands which have connected them with another, and to"; (3) line 3, "equal & independant" changed to "separate and equal"; (4) line 6, "the change" changed to "the separation"; (5) line 8, "& independant" deleted; (6) lines 8–9, "from that equal creation they derive rights" changed to "they are endowed by their creator with ["equal rights some of which are" struck out here in the process of making the correction]" and "rights; that" interlined after "inalienable"; (7) line 9, "which" changed to "these"; (8) line 9, "the preservation of" deleted; (9) line 10, "&" deleted; (10), "ends" changed to "rights"; (11) line 13, "shall" deleted and "s" added to "become"; (12) line 23, "power" changed to "Despotism"; (13) line 27, "his" changed to "the" and "Majesty" changed to "King of Great Britain"; (14) line 28, "no one fact stands single or solitary" changed to "appears no solitary fact."

Page Two of the Rough Draft: (15) at lines 9 and 10, on the slip pasted in by Jefferson is written: "he has called together legislative bodies at places unusual, uncomfortable, & distant from the depository of their public records, for the sole purpose of fatiguing them into compliance with his measures."[53] This is the first of three paragraphs inserted in the text by Jefferson during this phase of its development. (16) line 20, "colonies" changed to "states";[54] (17) line 22, "and amount of their salaries" changed to read "and the amount & payment of their salaries";[55]

(18) line 25, "without our consent" interlined after "peace" and then struck out; "without ["our" struck out here in process of making the change] the consent of our Legislatures"; (19) lines 28–29, "acts of" deleted after "pretended" and inserted after "their"; (20) line 31, "which" inserted before "they";[56] (21) below line 35, at the very bottom of the page, Jefferson has inserted the second of the new paragraphs mentioned above: "for abolishing the free system of English laws in a neighboring province, establishing therein an arbitrary government and enlarging it's boundaries so as to render it at once an example & fit instrument for introducing the same absolute rule into these colonies."[57]

Page Three of the Rough Draft: (22) line 1, "abolishing our most ["important" struck out in process of making the change] valuable Laws" inserted after "charters"; (23) line 8, "Scotch and other" inserted after "armies of";[58] (24) above line 16: this is the third of the new paragraphs inserted at this stage of the development of the draft, but whereas Jefferson had placed it immediately below the paragraph beginning "he has incited," Congress changed the sequence and put it below the paragraph beginning "he is at this time"—at which place Jefferson started to insert it and immediately below line ten he wrote the phrase "he has constrained c[S][?]" and then stopped. The new paragraph as inserted by Jefferson reads: "he has constrained others[59] ["falling into his hands" was struck out in process of composing the paragraph] taken captive on the high seas to bear arms against their country ["& to destroy & be destroyed by the brethren whom they love," struck out in process of composition] to become the executioners of their friends & brethren or to fall themselves by their hands"; (25) line 31, "only" inserted after "answered"; (26) line 35, "on so many acts of tyranny without a mask" struck out and "to ["lay" deleted in process of making the change] build a foundation so broad & undisguised, for tyranny" substituted; (27) line 36, "liberty" changed to "freedom."

Page Four of the Rough Draft: (28) line 12, "& connection" struck out after, and "connection &" inserted before, "correspondence"; (29) line 17, "deluge us in blood" struck out and "destroy us" inserted; (30) line 30, "& break off" deleted; (31) line 30, "have" deleted before, and inserted after, "heretofore"; (32) line 33, "shall hereafter" deleted and "full" inserted after "have."

These, in substance, are the changes made in the draft of the Declaration before it was submitted to Congress. For the most part they were verbal changes, the three new paragraphs added by Jefferson—unless Adams or Franklin suggested one or more of them—being the most significant alterations, and these paragraphs may very well have been inserted by Jefferson after he received the Rough Draft back from Adams and Franklin. It will be seen that what the members of the Committee did to the draft was trifling compared to the emasculation it suffered at the hands of Congress. The change attributed by Jefferson to Adams in this phase of the draft is that detailed above in item (13); those accredited to Franklin by Jefferson's marginalia in the Rough Draft are items (12), (17), (22), (25) and (29).

FROM THIS POINT ON IT IS FAIRLY SIMPLE to tell what happened to the Declaration in the third stage of its evolution, for Jefferson himself was careful to describe that process of alteration. The Committee of Five reported on Friday, June 28 and Congress properly laid the draft on the table, since the Richard Henry Lee Resolution of Independence had not yet been adopted and was scheduled for the debate on the following Monday. On July 2 the Committee of the Whole reported in favor of the first paragraph of the Lee Resolution—the part respecting independence—and Congress adopted the report, thereby officially separating the colonies from the British Empire. Having taken this action in the early part of that "fine clear & very cool morning" in Philadelphia, the Congress immediately resolved itself again into the Committee of the Whole in order to consider the draft of the Declaration that the Committee of Five had reported. The text was discussed by Congress all of the remainder of that day, all of July 3, and most of July 4, while Jefferson with an author's sensitive eyes suffered as he saw one of America's greatest literary achievements subjected to Congressional surgery. Some of the changes were undoubtedly necessary, viewed in the light of exigent realities, for Congress was faced with the problem of maintaining united councils and the unanimity so boldly proclaimed in the title which Congress gave to the Declaration was by no means apparent in the halls of the legislature or among the people. On the whole, therefore, Congress, with some very compelling reasons—notably in its refusal to inject the issue of the slave trade into an already hazardous situation and in its refusal to indict the English people for the faults of their King and his ministers—was much more lenient with the literary qualities of the noble document than some in the nineteenth century, who with far less cause and speaking for a less idealistic generation, spoke of its "glittering and sounding generalities." Moreover, it seems obvious that in some cases the changes made in Congress not only made the Declaration more adroit politically but actually improved the force and simplicity of the language.

The changes made in the Declaration by Congress, as indicated in the Madison, Richard Henry Lee, and Cassius F. Lee copies, in the Rough Draft and in the copy in Jefferson's *Notes*, may now be listed. There is not included in this list a change that apparently was contemplated by Congress, but not made. This was the question of the elimination of the word "General" from the title "A Declaration by the Representatives of the United States of America in General Congress Assembled." Someone in Congress may have suggested that this word should be struck out, for Jefferson underlined it in the Cassius F. Lee copy and in the copy in his *Notes* and both underlined and bracketed the word in the Madison copy. But neither the Rough Draft nor the Richard Henry Lee copy nor the Washburn copy bears any such marking. The suggestion in Congress, if made, was probably withdrawn.

Page One of the Rough Draft: (1) line 9, "inherent &" changed to "certain" and "inalienable" changed to "unalienable." This alteration may possibly have been made by the printer rather than at the suggestion of Congress. The Rough Draft reads "inalienable" without any indication of change made in Congress. None of the copies made by Jefferson has the form "unalienable," and none save the Richard Henry Lee copy indicates that "inalienable" was changed to "unalienable" in Congress, and, according to its endorsement, the indication in the margin of that copy of changes that took place in Congress was made not by Jefferson but by Arthur Lee. The copy printed by Dunlap and inserted in the Rough Journal of Congress is the first official copy that has the form "unalienable," though it will be noticed that the copy taken by John Adams used that spelling. Both forms were apparently current in the eighteenth century but, since this is the only change in Jefferson's spelling made by Congress—or by any of the Committee—and since none of Jefferson's copies indicate a change made by Congress, it may possibly be that we are indebted to John Dunlap, or a faulty proofreader, for this one.[60] (2) line 21, "begun at a distinguished period, &" deleted; (3) line 26, "expunge" changed to "alter"; (4) line 27, "unremitting" changed to "repeated"; (5) lines 28–29, "among which appears no solitary fact to contradict the uniform tenor of the rest, but all have" deleted and "all having" inserted at this point; (6) lines 31–32, "for the truth of which we pledge a faith yet unsullied by falsehood" deleted.

Page Two of the Rough Draft: (7) line 5, "utterly" deleted after and inserted before "neglected";[61] (8) line 9, "and continually" deleted; (9) line 19, "suffered" deleted and "obstructed" inserted; (10) lines 19–20, "totally to cease in some of these states" deleted, and "by" inserted; (11) line 21, "our" deleted; (12) line 23, "by a self-assumed power," deleted—a change which was indubitably an improvement in style without sacrifice of force or meaning; (13) line 25, "& ships of war" deleted; (14) line 34, "in many cases" inserted after "us"; (15) last line of new paragraph inserted by Jefferson, as indicated above, and last two words on page two of the Rough Draft: "colonies" changed to "states." [62]

Page Three of the Rough Draft: (16) lines 4–5, "withdrawing his governors, & declaring us out of his allegiance & protection:" deleted and "by declaring us out of his protection & waging war against us" —another effective change in language; (17) line 10, "scarcely paralleled in the most barbarous ages and totally" inserted after "perfidy"; (18) line 11, "excited domestic insurrections amongst us and has" inserted after "he has"; (19) line 13, "of existence" deleted after "conditions"; (20) lines 14–15, he has incited treasonable insurrections of our fellow-citizens,[63] with the allurements of forfeiture & confiscation of our property" deleted; (21) lines 16 to 29— the indictment against the King respecting the slave trade—deleted; (22) line 33, "free" inserted before "people"; (23) lines 33 to 36, everything after the word "people" on line 33 to the bottom of the page deleted.

Page Four of the Rough Draft: (24) line 2, "a" deleted and "an unwarranted" inserted after "extend"; (25) line 3, "these our states" changed to "us"; (26) lines 4 to 10, after "settlement here," the following passage deleted: "no one of which could warrant so strange a pretension: that these were effected at the expence of our own blood & treasure, unassisted by the wealth or the strength of Great Britain: that in constituting indeed our several forms of government, we had adopted one common king, thereby laying a foundation for perpetual league & amity with them: but that submission to their parliament was no part of our constitution, nor ever in idea, if history may be credited: and"; (27) line 10, "have" inserted after "we"; (28) line 10, "as well as to" deleted and "and we have conjured them by" inserted; (29) line 11, "were likely to" changed to "would inevitably"; (30) lines 13–24, the following deleted: "& when occasions have been given them, by the regular course of their laws, of removing from their councils the disturbers of our harmony, they have by their free election reestablished them in power, at this very time too they are permitting their chief magistrate to send over not only soldiers of our common blood, but Scotch & foreign mercenaries to invade & destroy us, these facts have given the last state to agonizing affection, and manly spirit bids us to renounce forever these unfeeling brethren, we must endeavor to forget our former love for them, and to hold them as we hold the rest of mankind, enemies in war, in peace friends, we might have been a free & great people together; but a communication of grandeur & of freedom it seems is below their dignity, be it so, since they will have it: the road to happiness & to glory is open to us too; we will climb it apart from them, and". There is one interesting point here indicating that Congress made one minor change before striking out the whole passage, though retaining the finest sentence in it. This minor change occurs in line 23; "climb" was deleted and "must tread" inserted, then "must" was also struck out. This was almost certainly done in Congress, for both the Richard Henry Lee and the Cassius F. Lee copies have "climb" whereas the copy in Jefferson's *Notes*—and, of course, the copy made therefrom for Madison—has "tread"; (31) lines 13 and 24, "We must therefore" inserted at the beginning of the deleted passage at line 13, having been begun at line 24 and then rubbed over apparently when the ink was still wet, and the following taken out of the deleted passage and inserted after "separation" : "and hold them as we hold the rest of mankind, enemies in war, in peace friends"; (32) line 27, "appealing to the supreme judge of the world for the rectitude of our intentions" inserted after "assembled"; (33) lines 27–30, "states, reject and renounce all allegiance & subjection to the kings of Great Britain & all others who may hereafter claim by, through, or under them; we utterly dissolve" changed to read "colonies, solemnly publish & declare that these United colonies are & of right ought to be free & independant states; that they are absolved from all allegiance to the British Crown, and that"; (34) line 30, "which may heretofore have subsisted" deleted; (35) line 31 "us" changed to "them"; (36) line 31, "people or parliament" changed to "state"; (37) line 31, "is & ought to be totally dissolved;" inserted after "Great Britain"; (38) lines 31 and 32, "and finally we do assert and declare these colonies to be free and independant states," deleted; (39) line 36, "with a firm reliance on the protection of divine providence," deleted.

FROM THE BRIEF SUMMARY OF THE TEXTUAL EVOLUTION of the Declaration of Independence it thus appears that, both numerically and quantitatively, Congress eliminated more and added fewer words to the Declaration than any or all of the Committee of Five. In the first stage of the progress of the Declaration, fifteen alterations were made; in the second, thirty-two; and in the third, thirty-nine. This was to be expected. Jefferson and his colleagues on the Committee were only five in number and two of these, if we may credit Jefferson's statement, made no alterations in the document. On the other hand Congress was a fairly numerous body and included some men of very acute intelligence. "I am among a Consistory of Kings … an August Assembly," Abraham Baldwin of New Jersey wrote on the very day that scholars such as James Wilson and John Witherspoon focussed their keen minds on Jefferson's supreme statement of American principles. It is difficult to point out a passage in the Declaration, great as it was, that was not improved by their attention. That a public body would reduce rather than increase the number of words in a political document is in itself a remarkable testimony to their sagacity and ability to express themselves. Certainly the final paragraph, considered as parliamentary practice, as political principle, and as literature was greatly improved by the changes of Congress. For as it was Jefferson's duty to build his justification upon the Resolution of Independence, it would seem to have been in order for him to reproduce, as Congress did, the precise words as well as the sense of that resolution. Moreover, having already denied the theory that Parliament had any jurisdiction over the colonies, he weakened the final statement by severing a political connection which he had claimed was not in existence. Congress made the statement politically stronger by assuming in great dignity that Parliament need not be mentioned, since, as the Declaration implied all the way through, the colonies acknowledged a constitutional tie only with the King and that was the only tie that needed to be severed in so solemn a proclamation.[64]

Jefferson, we know, was greatly disturbed by these excisions, as well he might have been no matter how excellent the alterations. The wise and understanding Franklin, sitting next to him, soothed his lacerated feelings by telling him the now famous story of John Thompson, the hatter, whose signboard before his shop bore the legend "John Thompson, Hatter, makes and sells hats for ready money" which, under the advice of critical friends, finally was reduced to "John Thompson" with the figure of a hat subjoined. This kindly act on Franklin's part may have helped, but Jefferson's wounded feelings were evidenced in the next few days when he sent to various friends copies of his Declaration as it stood before Congress altered it. It must have pleased him when Richard Henry Lee replied, after examining both Jefferson's earlier draft and the Declaration as finally adopted by Congress: "I wish sincerely, as well for the honor of Congress, as for that of the States, that the Manuscript had not been mangled as it is." John Adams was pleased with the paragraph about slavery, but he implied that he thought its language somewhat too dramatic when he said that Congress had struck out some of the most "oratorical" passages of the Declaration. Jefferson explained that his condemnation of the slave trade was "struck out in complaisance to S. Carolina & Georgia, who had never attempted to restrain the importation of slaves & who on the contrary still wished to continue it. Our northern brethren also, I believe, felt a little tender under those censures; for tho' their people have very few slaves themselves, yet they had been pretty considerable carriers of them to others." Also, Jefferson explained, "the pusillanimous idea that we had friends in England worth keeping terms with still haunted the minds of many," and for this reason "those passages which conveyed censures on the people of England were struck out lest they should give them offence."[65]

Immediately after the Declaration had been approved, Congress ordered that it be authenticated and printed. John Hancock signed this authenticated copy—perhaps the fair copy in Jefferson's handwriting that the Committee of Five had reported to Congress—"by Order and in Behalf of the Congress," Charles Thomson attested it, and the Committee of Five was ordered to "superintend & correct the press." It may be that Jefferson, as chairman of the Committee, took the authenticated copy to John Dunlap—perhaps, it is pleasant to suppose, accompanied by the greatest of all colonial printers—and watched over its composition and proofs during the night of July 4. But even Franklin could not have given more appropriate setting to the calm majesty of Jefferson's cadences than the chaste broadside that John Dunlap printed. It was not until July 19 that Congress ordered the Declaration engrossed on parchment, with the title changed to "The Unanimous Declaration of the 13 United States of America." The Journal, for August 2, 1776, bears this entry: "The declaration of Independence being engrossed & compared at the table was signed by the Members." It is well known that the famous copy on parchment was not signed by all those who voted for the measure on July 4; that some of those who signed it were not present in Congress on July 4 to vote upon its adoption; and that not all of those who signed did so on August 2.[66]

If this analysis of the evolution of the text suggests anything, it is that the charter of American liberty, far from being brought full-blown into the world, was the result not merely of a single author's lonely struggle for the right phrase and the telling point, but also of the focussing of many minds—among them a few of the best that America ever produced—upon this world-famous proclamation. Embodied in its fire-tested text are the phrases as well as the ideas that stirred the American mind and spirit of that and subsequent generations. It is the embodiment of what Americans were saying in countless sermons, speeches, pamphlets, letters, and conversations—even in their last wills and testaments. "I give my son," Josiah Quincy wrote into his will in 1774, "when he shall arrive at the age of 15 years, Algernon Sidney's Works, John Locke's Works, Lord Bacon's Works, Gordon's Tacitus, and Cato's Letters. May the spirit of Liberty rest upon him!" This was a noble legacy and a timeless exhortation. What Quincy willed to his son, Jefferson and his compatriots left as a legacy to all mankind, expressing in immortal phrases the idea that liberty and self-government were realities for which men would gladly sacrifice their lives, their fortunes, and their sacred honor. We owe this great document not merely to the young Virginian who, at thirty-three, was already committed to "eternal hostility against every form of tyranny over the mind of man," but also to a whole generation of men who dared to embrace the stern right of revolution and to proclaim to their world and to posterity the high reasons for their daring.

Jefferson's Drafts of
The Declaration of Independence

AND RELATED DOCUMENTS IN PHOTOREPRODUCTION

Document I

George Mason's Draft of the Virginia Bill of Rights, 1776

Reproduced from the earliest known draft of the Declaration of Rights, which became a part of the Virginia Constitution of 1776. In the handwriting of George Mason and Thomas Ludwell Lee, and showing on its fourth page especially the early form of some of the articles as discussed by the committee of the Virginia Convention. From the papers of George Mason in the Library of Congress. A copy of this first draft, endorsed by Mason as such, was presented by General John Mason in 1844 to the State of Virginia and is to be found in the State Library at Richmond. This copy is reproduced in Kate Mason Rowland, *Life of George Mason,* I, 240. In 1778 Mason wrote to George Mercer in London: "This was the first thing of its kind upon the continent, and has been closely imitated by all the States"; *ibid.,* I, 237. The question of its influence on Jefferson's Declaration of Independence has been much discussed. <In the 1943 edition> this document is reproduced in actual size , as are all of the following, save Document X.

Papers of George Mason, Manuscript Division, Library of Congress.

A Declaration of Rights, made by the Represen=tatives of the good People of Virginia, assembled in full Convention; and recommended to Posterity as the Basis and Foundation of their Government.

That all men are equally free and independent, and have certain inherent natural Rights, of which they can not, by any Compact, deprive or divest their Posterity; among which are the Enjoyment of Life and Liberty, with the Means of acquiring and possessing Property, and pursuing and obtaining Happiness and Safety.

That Power is, by God and Nature, vested in, and consequently derived from, the People; that Magistrates are their Trustees and Servants, and at all times amenable to them.

That Government is, or ought to be, instituted for the common Benefit and Security of the People, Nation, or Community. Of all the various Modes and Forms of Government, that is best which is capable of producing the greatest Degree of Happiness and Safety, and is most effectually secured against the Danger of mal-administration; and that whenever any Government shall be found inadequate or contrary to these Purposes, a Majority of the Community hath an indubitable, inalienable, and indefeasible Right to reform, alter, or abolish it, in such Manner as shall be judged most conducive to the Public Weal.

2

That no Man, or Set of Men are entitled to exclusive or separate Emoluments or Privileges from the Community, but in Consideration of public Services; which not being descendible, or hereditary, the Idea of a Man born a Magistrate, a Legislator, or a Judge is unnatural and absurd.

That the legislative and executive Powers of the State should be separate and distinct from the Judicative; and that the Members of the two first may be restrained from Oppression, by feeling and participating the Burthens they may lay upon the People; they should, at fixed Periods be reduced to a private Station, and returned, by frequent, certain and regular Elections, into that Body from which they were taken.

That no part of a Man's Property can be taken from him, or applied to public Uses, without the Consent of himself, or his legal Representatives; nor are the People bound by any Laws, but such as they have in like Manner, assented to, for their common Good.

That in all capital or criminal Prosecutions, a Man hath a Right to demand the Cause and Nature of his Accusation, to be confronted with the Accusers and Witnesses, to call for Evidence in his favour, and to a speedy Tryal by an impartial Jury of his Vicinage, without whose unanimous Consent he cannot be found guilty, nor can he be compelled to give Evidence against himself; and that no Man be deprived of his Liberty, except by the Law of the Land, or the Judgement of his Peers.

DOCUMENT I. *George Mason's Draft of the Virginia Bill of Rights, page two*

That the freedom of the press, being the great bulwark of liberty, can never be restrained but in a despotic government.

That laws having a retrospect to crimes & punishing offences committed before the existence

DOCUMENT I. *George Mason's Draft of the Virginia Bill of Rights, page three*

of such laws, are generally dangerous, and ought to be
avoided.

N.B. It is proposed to make some alteration in this
last article when reported to the house. Perhaps
somewhat like the following

That all laws having a retrospect to crimes,
& punishing offences committed before the existence of such laws are dangerous, and ought to be
avoided, except in cases of great & evident necessity, when the safety of the state absolutely requires
them. — This is thought to state with more
precision the doctrine respecting ex post facto
laws & to signify to posterity that it is considered not
so much as a law of right, as the great law of
necessity, which by a well known maxim is
allowed to supersede all human institutions.

Another is agreed to in committee condemning
the use of general warrants; & one other to prevent
the suspension of laws, or the execution of
them.

The above clauses, with some small alterations, & the addition of one or two more, have
already been agreed to in the committee
appointed to prepare a declaration of rights;
when this business is finished in the house, the
committee will proceed to the ordinance of government.   T.L. Lee —

DOCUMENT I. *George Mason's Draft of the Virginia Bill of Rights, page four*

Document II

Jefferson's "First Ideas" on the Virginia Constitution, 1776

Reproduced from the first two pages of the first of three drafts of a constitution which Jefferson sent to the Virginia Convention. From the original in the Jefferson papers in the Library of Congress. The Library also has another copy, lacking the part reproduced here, which was a list of reasons for Virginia's repudiation of her allegiance to George III and which was not only incorporated in large part in the Virginia Constitution as its Preamble but also followed closely by Jefferson in the corresponding part of the Declaration of Independence. The first draft is made up of six folio pages, being similar to another draft, likewise in Jefferson's handwriting, in the New York Public Library. The second draft was first published in *Writings of Thomas Jefferson,* P. L. Ford, ed., II, 7ff. The third copy, lacking the part contained in the two pages reproduced here, was presented to the Library of Congress in 1931. Both this copy and that in the New York Public Library came from Cassius F. Lee of Alexandria, Virginia. These drafts were probably written in the spring of 1776, and certainly before June 13, but there is no documentary evidence for supposing, as Fitzpatrick does, that they were drawn up after May 27; John C. Fitzpatrick, *Spirit of the American Revolution,* p. 2; see also, John H. Hazelton, *The Declaration of Independence,* New York, 1906, p. 146, 451–52. The first draft, reproduced <in 1943> in actual size, is on a paper manufactured in Holland and bearing the watermark L V G [errevink?], which is different from the paper used by Jefferson in his various drafts of the Declaration, thereby lending strength to the supposition of a somewhat earlier composition than Fitzpatrick indicates.

Papers of Thomas Jefferson, Manuscript Division, Library of Congress.

whereas George [...] Guelph king of Great Britain & Ireland &

Elector of Hanover, heretofore entrusted with the exercise of the kingly office in this government

hath endeavored to pervert the same into a detestable & insupportable tyranny

1. by putting his negative on laws the most wholesome & necessary for the public good

2. by denying to his governors permission to pass laws of [...] immediate & pressing im-

portance, unless suspended in their operation for his assent & when so suspended

neglecting [...] to attend to them for many years:

3. by refusing to pass certain other laws unless the persons to be benefited by them would

relinquish the inestimable right of representation in the legislature

4. by dissolving legislative assemblies repeatedly & continually for opposing with manly firm-

ness his invasions on the rights of the people:

5. when dissolved, by refusing to call others for a long space of time, thereby leaving the poli-

tical system [...] without any legislative body head.

6. by endeavoring to prevent the population of our country & obstructing the laws for

naturalization of foreigners & raising the conditions of appropriations of lands.

7. by keeping among us in times of peace standing armies & ships of war:

8. by affecting to render the military independent of & superior to the civil power:

9. by combining with others to subject us to a foreign jurisdiction giving his assent

their pretended acts of legislation [...] taxes on us without our consent

a. for quartering large bodies of armed troops among us & protect them [...] murders

[...] our trade with all parts of the world.

c. for imposing taxes on us without our consent

d. for depriving us of the benefits of trial by jury

e. for transporting us beyond seas to be tried for pretended offences

for taking away our charters & altering fundamentally the forms of our governments

f. for suspending our own legislatures & declaring themselves invested with power

to legislate for us in all cases whatsoever

10. by plundering our seas, ravaging our coasts, burning our towns, & destroying the lives

of our people.

11. by inciting insurrections of our fellow citizens with the allurements of forfeiture & confiscation

12. by prompting our negroes to rise in arms among us; those very negroes whom he hath by an inhuman use of his negative

refused us permission to exclude by law:

13. by endeavouring to bring on the inhabitants of our frontiers the merciless Indian savages

whose known rule of warfare is an undistinguished destruction of all ages, sexes, & conditions.

14. by transporting at this time a large army of foreign mercenaries to compleat the works of

death, desolation, & tyranny already begun with circumstances of cruelty & perfidy so unworthy the head of a civilized nation

15. by answering our repeated petitions with a repetition of injuries:

16. and finally by abandoning the helm of government & declaring us out of his allegiance & protection

[...]

office & divested of all it's privileges, powers, & prerogatives.

And forasmuch as the public liberty may be more [...] secured [...] an office

which all experience hath shewn to be inveterately inimical thereto [...]

necessary to re-establish such ancient principles as are friendly to the rights of the people & to declare

certain others which may [...] operate with & fortify the same in future

DOCUMENT II. *Jefferson's "First Ideas" on the Virginia Constitution, page one*

And whereas by an act of — — of the present parliament of Great Britain passed for the purpose of prohibiting all trade & intercourse with the colonies of New Hampshire, Massachusets bay, Rhode Island, Connecticut, New York, New Jersey, Pennsylvania, the three lower counties on Delaware, Maryland, Virginia, North Carolina, South Carolina, & Georgia it is declared that the said colonies are in a state of open Rebellion & hostility against the king & his parliament of Great Britain, that they are out of their allegiance to him & are thereby also put of his protection: and ~~now~~ it is further declared ~~in the said act~~ that as divers persons within the sd colonies may have been destroyed for the publick service in withstanding or suppressing the said rebellion, it is therefore enacted 'that all such acts shall be deemed just & legal to all intents ~~& purposes~~ constructions & purposes' to which act the sd George Guelph hath given his assent & thereby put us out of his allegiance & protection.; in which case it is provided by the original charter of compact granted to Sr Walter Raleigh on behalf of himself & the settlers of this colony & bearing date the 25th day of March 1584 'that if the said Walter Raleigh his heirs or assigns or any of them 'or any other by their licence or appointment should at any time thereafter 'do any act of unjust or unlawful hostility, to any of the subjects of the sd queen it should be lawful to the sd queen her heirs & successors 'her heirs or successors, to put the sd Walter Raleigh his heirs and assigns 'and adherents & all the inhabitants of the said places to be discovered as is there-'in described, or any of them out of her allegiance & protection; and that from '& after such time of putting out of protection of the said Walter Raleigh his heirs 'assigns & adherents & others so to be put out, & the sd places within their ha-'bitation prossession & rule, should be out of her allegiance & protection & free 'for all princes & others to pursue with hostility, as being not her subjects, nor 'by her any way to be avouched maintained or defended, nor to be holden as 'any of hers, nor to her protection or dominion or allegiance any way belonging' is that the sd George Guelph having by the said act of parliament declared us in a state of Rebellion & hostility, & put us out of his allegiance & protection, it follows by the sd charter that, from & after the time of such putting out, ourselves, and the places within our habitation, prossession & rule are not subject to him, & are not to be holden as any of his, nor to his dominion any way belonging.

From all which premisses it appears that the sd George Guelph, not only for his criminal abuses of the high duties of the kingly office, but also by his own free & voluntary act of abandoning & putting us from his allegiance subjection & dominion, may now lawfully, rightfully, & by consent of both par-ties be divested of the kingly powers:

DOCUMENT II. *Jefferson's "First Ideas" on the Virginia Constitution, page two*

Document III

Richard Henry Lee Resolution of Independence

Reproduced from the original in the Continental Congress Papers. It is in the handwriting of Richard Henry Lee who introduced it on June 7, acting on instructions of the Virginia Convention adopted May 15. It is written on the same kind of paper used by Jefferson in his various drafts, though the Lee resolution is on a half-sheet. The verso contains an endorsement in the handwriting of Charles Thomson, secretary of Congress; a report of the committee of the whole of June 10 recommending the appointment of a committee, in the handwriting of Benjamin Harrison; and an addition to this report, explaining the reasons for it, in the handwriting of Robert R. Livingston of New York. See Hazelton, *op. cit.*, 109–122. The resolution was adopted July 2 and it was Jefferson's duty in drawing up the Declaration to justify this formal vote of separation from Great Britain. It is worth noting that Jefferson did not adhere to the exact terms of the Lee Resolution in the final words of the Declaration, but Congress restored them.

Papers of the Continental Congress, National Archives and Records Administration.

: Resolved ~~the ~~

That these United Colonies are, and of right ought to be, free and independent States, that they are absolved from all allegiance to the British Crown, and that all political connection between them and the State of Great Britain is, and ought to be, totally dissolved.

That it is expedient forthwith to take the most effectual measures for forming foreign Alliances.

That a plan of confederation be prepared and transmitted to the respective Colonies for their consideration and approbation.

DOCUMENT III. *Richard Henry Lee Resolution of Independence, page one*

Resolved that it is the opinion of this Com. that the first resolution be postponed to this day three weeks, and that in the mean time, a committee be appointed to prepare a Declaration to the effect of the said first resolution.

+ least any time sh.ᵈ be lost in case the Congress agree to this resolution.

respecting R.H. Lees own

Resolution moved June 7. 1776. reported for consideration till to morrow

DOCUMENT III. *Richard Henry Lee Resolution of Independence, page two*

Fragment of the Earliest Known Draft of the Declaration of Independence, Written by Thomas Jefferson in June 1776

Reproduced from the original holograph manuscript in the Thomas Jefferson Papers in the Library of Congress. This manuscript in Thomas Jefferson's hand is the only known surviving fragment of the earliest identified draft of the Declaration of Independence. Although it represents only a small section of the text of the Declaration, this fragment demonstrates that Jefferson himself heavily edited at least one draft of the Declaration of Independence before he prepared a clean copy. Thus, it was this "fair copy" that became the basis of the "original Rough draught," the document first submitted to John Adams and Benjamin Franklin.

This fragment remained unrecognized in the Jefferson Papers until 1947 when it was identified by Julian P. Boyd, who was gathering material for the first volume of what has become a monumental edition of Jefferson's papers. The writing on the bottom half of the sheet is Jefferson's July 1776 draft resolution regarding the resignation General John Sullivan proffered Congress in reaction to the insult he felt when Congress appointed General Horatio Gates commander of American forces in Canada. On the verso of the sheet are Jefferson's pencil notes for a horse stall, apparently based on the stable of former Pennsylvania governor John Penn. Unfortunately, there is no visible complete or fragmentary watermark on this piece of paper.

An analysis of the text of this document fragment is very useful to our understanding of the process of drafting the Declaration of Independence. Half of the first line of text after "in po[wer]" is missing along the broken top edge of the manuscript. Benjamin Franklin, examining the text after Jefferson wrote it, deleted the phrase "deluge us in blood," replacing it with the words "destroy us," which were the same as those originally written by Jefferson in lines two and three of this composition draft. The phrase "in a separate state" in line eleven was first changed to "separately" by Jefferson in the "Rough Draft" and subsequently changed to "apart from them" in both this draft fragment and the "Rough Draft." John Adams' copy of the Declaration must have been made before the interdelineation of "apart from them." In line twelve Jefferson changed the word "pronounces" to "denounces" and the phrase "everlasting Adieu" to "eternal separation" in both the Rough Draft and the draft fragment. Adams also made on his copy these changes that were here completed by Jefferson. The alterations in lines eleven and twelve indicate that Jefferson continued to edit the Declaration even as he made his fair copy and that Franklin and Adams were intricately involved in the process. Lines thirteen and fourteen of this fragment were crossed out and interlined into the text of the paragraph above.

In order to focus attention on the transgression of the king and not the British people, Congress later deleted this entire paragraph from the final version of the Declaration of Independence, retaining only the phrase "acquiesce in the necessity, which denounces our separation" in lines eleven and twelve.

Papers of Thomas Jefferson, Manuscript Division, Library of Congress.

DOCUMENT IIIA. *Fragment of the earliest known draft of the Declaration of Independence, written by Thomas Jefferson in June 1776, page one*

DOCUMENT IIIA. *Fragment of the earliest known draft of the Declaration of Independence, written by Thomas Jefferson in June 1776, page two*

Document IV

John Adams' Copy of Jefferson's Original Draft

Reproduced from the original in the Adams family papers in the Massachusetts Historical Society, through the courtesy of the officers of the Adams Manuscript Trust, who also consented to have this extremely important document placed on exhibit in the current <1943> display of documents, books, and memorabilia of Thomas Jefferson at the Library of Congress. It is written on the same kind of paper as that used by Jefferson, as described in "The Drafting of the Declaration of Independence." Hazelton, *op. cit.,* p. 348–49, thinks this is probably the copy that John Adams sent to his wife, a plausible inference. If so, the present is probably the first occasion on which it has been out of the custody of the Adams family, a fact which, because of its importance in understanding the evolution of Jefferson's Rough Draft, is gratefully acknowledged. This <the 1943 edition> is also the first time it has been reproduced in facsimile. Adams made this copy after June 11 and before June 28, in all probability before the Rough Draft of Jefferson was submitted to Franklin.

Courtesy Massachusetts Historical Society, Boston.

A Declaration by the Representatives of the United States of America in general Congress assembled

When in the Course of human Events it becomes necessary for a People to advance from that Subordination, in which they have hitherto remained, and to assume among the Powers of the Earth, the equal and independent Station to which the Laws of Nature and of Nature's God entitle them, a decent Respect to the opinions of Mankind requires that they should declare the Causes, which impell them to the Change.

We hold these Truths to be self evident; that all Men are created equal and independent; that from that equal Creation they derive Rights inherent and unalienable; among which are the Preservation of Life, and Liberty, and the Pursuit of Happiness; that to secure these Ends, Governments are instituted among Men, deriving their just Powers from the Consent of the governed; that whenever, any form of Government, shall become destructive of these Ends, it is the Right of the People to alter, or to abolish it, and to institute new Government, laying its Foundation on such Principles, and organizing its Powers in such Form, as to them shall seem most likely to effect their Safety and Happiness. Prudence indeed will dictate that Governments long established should not be changed for light and transient Causes: and accordingly all Experience hath shewn, that Mankind are more disposed to suffer, while Evils are sufferable, than to right themselves, by abolishing the Forms to which they are accustomed. But when a long Train of Abuses and Usurpations, begun at a distinguish'd Period, and pursuing invariably, the same Object, evinces a Design to reduce them under absolute Power, it is their Right, it is their Duty, to throw off such Government, and to provide new Guards for their future Security. Such has been the patient Sufferance of these Colonies; and such is now the Necessity, which constrains them to expunge their former Systems of Government. The History of his present Majesty, is a History of unremitting Injuries and Usurpations, among which no one Fact stands single or solitary to contradict the uniform Tenor of the rest, all of which have in direct object, the Establishment of an absolute Tyranny over these States. To prove this, let Facts be submitted to a candid World, for the Truth of which We pledge a Faith, as yet unsullied by Falshood.

He has refused his Assent to Laws, the most wholesome and necessary for the public Good.

He has forbidden his Governors to pass Laws of immediate and pressing Importance, unless suspended in their Operation, till his Assent should be obtained; and when so suspended he has neglected utterly to attend to them.

He has refused to pass other Laws for the Accommodation of large Districts of People, unless those People would relinquish the Right of Representation in the Legislature, a Right inestimable to them, and formidable to Tyrants only.

He has dissolved Representative Houses, repeatedly, and continually, for opposing with manly Firmness his Invasions, on the Rights of the People.

He has refused, for a long Space of Time after such Dissolutions, to cause others to be elected, whereby the legislative Powers, incapable of annihilation, have returned to the People at large for their Exercise, the State remaining in the mean Time, exposed to all the Dangers of Invasion, from without, and Convulsions within —

He has endeavoured to prevent the Population of these States; for that purpose obstructing the Laws for naturalization of Foreigners; refusing to pass others to encourage their Migrations hither; and raising the Conditions of new Appropriations of Lands.

He has suffered the Administration of Justice totally to cease in some of these Colonies, refusing his Assent to Laws for establishing judiciary Powers.

He has made our Judges dependent on his Will alone, for the Tenure of their Offices, and amount of their Salaries:

He has erected a Multitude of new Offices by a Self-assumed Power, and sent hither Swarms of Officers to harrass our People and eat out their Substance.

He has kept among us, in Times of Peace, Standing Armies and Ships of War.

He has affected to render the military, independent of, and superiour to, the civil Power:

He has combined with others to subject us to a Jurisdiction foreign to our Constitution and unacknowledged by our Laws; giving his Assent to their pretended Acts of Legislation; for quartering large Bodies of armed Troops among us; for protecting them by a Mock Tryal from Punishment for any Murders they should commit on the Inhabitants of these States; for cutting off our Trade with all Parts of the World; for imposing Taxes on us without our Consent; for depriving us of the Benefits of Trial by Jury; for transporting us beyond Seas to be tried for pretended Offences; for taking away our Charters, and altering fundamentally the Forms of our Governments; for suspending our own Legislatures and declaring themselves is vested with Power to legislate for us in all Cases whatsoever.

He has abdicated Government here, withdrawing his Governors, and declaring us, out of his Allegiance and Protection.

He has plundered our Seas, ravaged our Coasts, burnt our Towns, and destroyed the Lives of our People.

He is at this Time transporting large Armies of foreign Mercenaries to compleat the Works of death, Desolation, and Tyranny, already begun with Circumstances of Cruelty and Perfidy unworthy the Head of a civilized Nation.

He has endeavoured to bring on the Inhabitants of our Frontiers, the merciless Indian Savages, whose known Rule of Warfare is an undistinguished Destruction of all Ages, Sexes, and Conditions of existence.

He has incited treasonable Insurrections of our Fellow Citizens, with the allurement of Forfeiture and Confiscation of our Property.

He has waged cruel war against human Nature itself, violating its most sacred Rights of Life and Liberty in the Persons of a distant People who never offended him, captivating and carrying them into Slavery in another Hemisphere, or to incur miserable Death, in their Transportation thither. This piratical warfare, the opprobrium of infidel Powers, is the warfare of the Christian King of Great Britain. determined to

He has prostituted his Negative for Suppressing every legislative Attempt to prohibit or to restrain an execrable Commerce, determined to keep open a Markett where Men should be bought and Sold. and that this assemblage of Horrors might want no fact of distinguished Die

He is now exciting those very People to rise in Arms among us, and to purchase that Liberty of which he has deprived them, by murdering the People upon whom he also obtruded them: thus paying off, former Crimes committed against the Liberties of one People, with Crimes which he urges them to commit against the Lives of another.

In every Stage of these Oppressions we have petitioned for redress, in the most humble Terms. our repeated Petitions have been answered by repeated Injury. A Prince, whose Character is thus marked by every Act which may define a Tyrant, is unfit to be the Ruler of a People who mean to be free. — future Ages will scarce believe, that the Hardiness of one Man, adventured, within the short Compass of twelve years only, on so many Acts of Tyranny, without a Mask, over a People, fostered and fixed in the Principles of Liberty.

DOCUMENT IV. *John Adams' copy of Jefferson's Original Draft, page three*

Nor have we been wanting in Attentions to our British Brethren. We have warned them from Time to Time of attempts of their Legislature to extend a Jurisdiction over these our States. We have reminded them of the Circumstances of our Emigration and Settlement here, no one of which could warrant so strange a Pretension. That these were effected at the Expence of our own Blood and Treasure, unassisted by the Wealth or the Strength of Great Britain: that in constituting indeed, our several Forms of Government, we had adopted one common King, thereby laying a Foundation for perpetual League and Amity with them: but that Submission to their Parliament, was no Part of our Constitution, nor ever in Idea, if History may be credited: and we appealed to their Native Justice and Magnanimity, as well as to the Ties of our common Kindred to disavow these Usurpations, which were likely to interrupt our Correspondence and Connection. They too have been deaf to the Voice of Justice and of Consanguinity, and when occasions have been given them by the regular Course of their Laws of removing from their Councils, the Disturbers of our Harmony, they have by their free Election, re-established them in Power. At this very Time too, they are permitting their Chief Magistrate to send over not only Soldiers of our common Blood, but Scotch and foreign Mercenaries, to invade and deluge us in Blood. These Facts have given the last Stab to agonising Affection, and manly Spirit bids us to renounce forever these unfeeling Brethren. We must endeavour to forget our former Love for them, and to hold them, as we hold the rest of Mankind, Enemies in War, in Peace Friends. We might have been a free and a great People together; but a Communication of Grandeur and of Freedom it seems is below their Dignity. Be it so, since they will have it: The Road to Happiness and to Glory is open to us too; we will climb it, apart from them, and acquiesce in the Necessity which denounces our eternal Separation.!

We therefore the Representatives of the united States of America in General Congress assembled, do, in the Name, and by the Authority of the good People of these States, reject and renounce all Allegiance and Subjection to the Kings of Great Britain, and all others, who may hereafter claim by, through, or under them; we utterly dissolve and break off all political connection which may have heretofore subsisted between us and the People or Parliament of Great Britain, and finally we do assert and declare these Colonies to be free and independent States, and that as free and independant States they shall hereafter have Power to levy War, conclude Peace, contract Alliances, establish Commerce, and to do all other Acts and Things which independant States may of Right do. And for the Support of this Declaration, we mutually pledge to each other our Lives, our Fortunes, and our Sacred Honour.

DOCUMENT IV. *John Adams' copy of Jefferson's Original Draft, page four*

Jefferson's Rough Draft of the Declaration of Independence

Reproduced from the original in the Jefferson Papers in the Library of Congress. This great document represents the form in which Jefferson submitted it, together with all corrections, additions, and deletions made by Adams and Franklin, by the Committee of Five, and by the Congress. In the text Jefferson has enclosed in brackets those parts stricken out by Congress sitting as the committee of the whole. At a later date, perhaps in the nineteenth century, Jefferson indicated in the margins some, but not all, of the corrections suggested by Adams and Franklin. An earlier draft or preliminary notes probably preceded this, as is indicated by internal evidence, but this is not certainly known and no such draft has survived <except the fragment, Document IIIA>; see below and Hazelton, *op. cit.*, p. 345, 601. From this rough draft Jefferson is thought to have taken a fair copy for the Committee which he submitted to Congress. If so, Charles Thomson may have sent it to the printer as copy, thereby causing it to be lost. The Rough Draft has been reproduced in facsimile several times, an excellent reproduction being in Hazelton, p. 144, but this <the 1943 edition> is the first time that it has been reproduced to show the precise nature of the slip pasted onto page two by Jefferson and the first time it has been reproduced in association with all of the known copies made by Jefferson.

While no scientific photographic studies of watermarks in this and other drafts have been made, nor any tests of paper fibre, it is obvious to the layman that the Rough Draft and the copies reproduced as Documents IV, VI, VII, and IX are written on paper of the same kind made by the same manufacturer. The irregularly spaced bridge-marks correspond in all of these copies and the wire-marks run 22 to the inch in each of them. The paper is presumably of Holland manufacture and its watermark, bearing in a ribbon the device "Pro Patria Eiusque Libertate" is similar to, if not identical with that described by Fiske Kimball in his *Thomas Jefferson, Architect* (Boston, 1916), p. 113; *see also,* Del Marmol, *Dictionnaire des Filigranes* (Namur, 1900), p. 75. Dard Hunter, in his *Papermaking: The History and Technique of an Ancient Craft* (New York, 1943), p. 18, makes the statement that the paper of the Rough Draft bears on its second sheet the watermark L V G and that it was probably of Dutch manufacture by one of three prominent papermakers: Lubertus van Gerrevink of Egmond a.d.Hoef, Lucas van Gerrevink of Alkmaar, or L. van Groot (or van Grooten). Mr. Hunter has been misled as to the watermark in the Rough Draft, for neither it nor any other of the Jefferson copies contains on the first or second sheets the watermark L V G. All of them contain the "Pro Patria Eiusque Libertate" watermark on their first sheets as described above and all of their bridge-marks and wire-marks are as indicated. A letter from John C. Fitzpatrick to Carl Becker, dated July 26, 1924, gives the erroneous information that the second sheet contains the watermark L V G. This letter, a copy of which is in the Manuscripts Division of the Library of Congress, is doubtless the basis of subsequent statements made in behalf of the Library of Congress which misled Hunter and others.

Papers of Thomas Jefferson, Manuscript Division, Library of Congress.

A Declaration by the Representatives of the UNITED STATES OF AMERICA, in General Congress assembled.

When in the course of human events it becomes necessary for ~~one~~ people to dissolve the political bands which have connected them with another, and to ~~assume~~ among the powers of the earth the separate and equal station to which the laws of nature & of nature's god entitle them, a decent respect to the opinions of mankind requires that they should declare the causes which impel them to the separation.

We hold these truths to be self-evident; that all men are created equal, ~~& independent~~ that ~~from that equal creation they derive~~ they are endowed by their creator with ~~equal~~ inherent & inalienable rights; that among these are life, liberty, & the pursuit of happiness; that to secure these ~~rights~~, governments are instituted among men, deriving their just powers from the consent of the governed; that whenever any form of government shall becomes destructive of these ends, it is the right of the people to alter or to abolish it, & to institute new government, laying it's foundation on such principles & organising it's powers in such form, as to them shall seem most likely to effect their safety & happiness. prudence indeed will dictate that governments long established should not be changed for light & transient causes: and accordingly all experience hath shewn that mankind are more disposed to suffer while evils are sufferable, than to right themselves by abolishing the forms to which they are accustomed. but when a long train of abuses & usurpations [begun at a distinguished period, &] pursuing invariably the same object, evinces a design to ~~subject~~ reduce them + under absolute Despotism, it is their right, it is their duty, to throw off such + & to provide new guards for their future security. such has been the patient sufferance of these colonies; & such is now the necessity which constrains them to expunge their former systems of government. the history of the present king of Great Britain is a history of ~~unremitting~~ injuries and usurpations, [among which, appears no solitary fact ~~but all~~ to contradict the uniform tenor of the rest [all of which have] in direct object the establishment of an absolute tyranny over these states. to prove this, let facts be submitted to a candid world, for the truth of which we pledge a faith yet unsullied by falsehood.]

DOCUMENT V. *Jefferson's Rough Draft, page one*

he has refused his assent to laws the most wholesome and necessary for the pub-
-lic good:

he has forbidden his governors to pass laws of immediate & pressing importance,

unless suspended in their operation till his assent should be obtained;

and when so suspended, he has utterly neglected ~~entirely~~ to attend to them.

he has refused to pass other laws for the accomodation of large districts of people

unless those people would relinquish the right of representation in the legislature, a right

inestimable to them, & formidable to ~~tyrants~~ its only:

~~as dissolved Repre-~~ ~~-tive houses repeatedly & continually~~

manly firmness his invasions on the rights of the people:

~~he has dissolved~~, he has refused for a long ~~space~~ time after such dissolutions to cause others to be elected, *mr Adams

~~whereby the~~ legislative powers, incapable of annihilation, have returned to

the people at large for their exercise, the state remaining in the mean time

exposed to all the dangers of invasion from without & convulsions within:

~~he has~~ endeavored to prevent the population of these states; for that purpose

obstructing the laws for naturalization of foreigners; refusing to pass others

to encourage their migrations hither, & raising the conditions of new ap-

-propriations of lands:

he has ~~suffered~~ the ~~administration~~ of justice totally to cease in some of ~~these~~
~~states~~ ~~by~~ refusing his assent to laws for establishing judiciary powers:

he has made [our] judges dependant on his will alone, for the tenure of their offices,
the + & payment
and amount of their salaries: + Dr Franklin

he has erected a multitude of new offices [by a self-assumed power,] & sent hi-

-ther swarms of officers to harrass our people & eat out their substance:
~~in time of peace~~
he has kept among us in times of peace standing armies [& ships of war:] without the consent of our legislatures

he has affected to render the military, independent of & superior to the civil power:

~~he has combined with others to subject us to a jurisdiction foreign to our constitu-~~
-tions and unacknoleged by our laws; giving his assent to their acts of pretended ~~acts~~

& legislation, for quartering large bodies of armed troops among us;

for protecting them by a mock-trial from punishment for any murders
which
~~they~~ should commit on the inhabitants of these states;

for cutting off our trade with all parts of the world;

for imposing taxes on us without our consent;
in many cases
for depriving us of the benefits of trial by jury;

for transporting us beyond seas to be tried for pretended offences:
for abolishing the free system of English laws in a neighboring province, establishing therein an ar-
and enlarging it's boundaries so as to render it at once an example & fit instrument for introducing the

DOCUMENT V. *Jefferson's Rough Draft, page two, without the flap*

he has refused his assent to laws the most wholesome and necessary for the pub-
-lic good:

he has forbidden his governors to pass laws of immediate & pressing importance,

unless suspended in their operation till his assent should be obtained;

and when so suspended, he has utterly neglected utterly to attend to them.

he has refused to pass other laws for the accomodation of large districts of people

unless those people would relinquish the right of representation in the legislature, a right

inestimable to them & formidable to tyrants only:

he has called together legislative bodies at places unusual, unco-

-ble, & from the depository of their public records, for the sole purpose of fat-

with his measures:

time after such dissolutions &c

he has refused for a long space of time to cause others to be elected, * mr Adams

whereby the legislative powers, incapable of annihilation, have returned to

the people at large for their exercise, the state remaining in the mean time

exposed to all the dangers of invasion from without & convulsions within:

he has endeavored to prevent the population of these states; for that purpose

obstructing the laws for naturalization of foreigners; refusing to pass others

to encourage their migrations hither; & raising the conditions of new ap-

-propriations of lands:

he has suffered the administration of justice totally to cease in some of these

states, refusing his assent to laws for establishing judiciary powers:

he has made our judges dependant on his will alone, for the tenure of their offices,

the + & payment
and amount of their salaries: + Dr Franklin

he has erected a multitude of new offices [by a self-assumed power,] & sent hi-

ther swarms of officers to harrass our people & eat out their subsistance:

                                        without the consent of our   legislatures
he has kept among us in times of peace standing armies [& ships of war;]

he has affected to render the military independent of & superior to the civil power:

he has combined with others to subject us to a jurisdiction foreign to our constitu-

-tions and unacknoleged by our laws; giving his assent to their pretended acts of

legislation, for quartering large bodies of armed troops among us;

        for protecting them by a mock-trial from punishment for any murders
        which
        they should commit on the inhabitants of these states;

        for cutting off our trade with all parts of the world;

        for imposing taxes on us without our consent;
                            in many cases
        for depriving us of the benefits of trial by jury;

        for transporting us beyond seas to be tried for pretended offences:
        for abolishing the free system of English laws in a neighboring province, establishing therein an arbitrary government,
        and enlarging it's boundaries so as to render it at once an example & fit instrument for introducing the same absolute
        rule into these colonies

DOCUMENT V. *Jefferson's Rough Draft, page two, with the paste-on flap*

abolishing our most valuable important Laws

for taking away our charters & altering fundamentally the forms of our governments,

for suspending our own legislatures & declaring themselves invested with power to

legislate for us in all cases whatsoever.

he has abdicated government here, [withdrawing his governors, & declaring us out of his allegiance & protection:] by declaring us out of his protection & waging war against us.

he has plundered our seas, ravaged our coasts, burnt our towns & destroyed the lives of our people:

he is at this time transporting large armies of foreign mercenaries to compleat the works of death, desolation & tyranny already begun with circumstances of cruelty & perfidy, unworthy the head of a civilized nation: Scotch and other scarcely paralleled in the most barbarous ages, & totally

he has endeavored to bring on the inhabitants of our frontiers the merciless Indian savages, whose known rule of warfare is an undistinguished destruction of all ages, sexes, & conditions [of existence:]

[he has incited treasonable insurrections of our fellow-citizens, with the allurements of forfeiture & confiscation of our property:

he has waged cruel war against human nature itself, violating it's most sacred rights of life & liberty in the persons of a distant people who never offended him, captivating & carrying them into slavery in another hemisphere, or to incur miserable death in their transportation thither. this piratical warfare, the opprobrium of infidel powers, is the warfare of the Christian king of Great Britain. determined to keep open a market where MEN should be bought & sold, he has prostituted his negative for suppressing every legislative attempt to prohibit or to restrain this execrable commerce: and that this assemblage of horrors might want no fact of distinguished die, he is now exciting those very people to rise in arms among us, and to purchase that liberty of which he has deprived them, by murdering the people upon whom he also obtruded them: thus paying off former crimes committed against the liberties of one people, with crimes which he urges them to commit against the lives of another.]

in every stage of these oppressions' we have petitioned for redress' in the most humble terms''; our repeated petitions' have been answered only by repeated injuries''. a prince whose character is thus marked by every act which may define a tyrant,' is unfit to be the ruler of a people [who mean to be free''. future ages will scarce believe' that the hardiness of one man'' adventured within the short compass' of twelve years only to lay a foundation so broad & undisguised; for tyranny over a people fostered & fixed in principles of freedom.]

DOCUMENT V. *Jefferson's Rough Draft, page three*

Nor have we been wanting in attentions to our British brethren. we have warned them from time to time of attempts by their legislature to extend a jurisdiction over [these our states]. we have reminded them of the circumstances of our emigration & settlement here, no one of which could warrant so strange a pretension: that these were effected at the expence of our own blood & treasure, unassisted by the wealth or the strength of Great Britain: that in constituting indeed our several forms of government, we had adopted one common king, thereby laying a foundation for perpetual league & amity with them: but that submission to their

credited: and we appealed to their native justice & magnanimity, as well as to the ties of our common kindred to disavow these usurpations which were likely to interrupt our connection & correspondence. they too have been deaf to the voice of justice & of consanguinity, & when occasions have been given them, by the regular course of their laws, of removing from their councils the disturbers of our harmony, they have by their free election re-established them in power. at this very time too they are permitting their chief magistrate to send over not only soldiers of our common blood, but Scotch & foreign mercenaries to invade & destroy us. these facts

have unfeeling brethren. we must endeavor to forget our former love for them, and to hold them as we hold the rest of mankind, enemies in war, in peace friends. we might have been a free & a great people together; but a communication of grandeur & of freedom it seems is below their dignity. be it so, since they will have it: the road to happiness & to glory is open to us too; we will tread it apart from them, and acquiesce in the necessity which denounces our [eternal] separation!

We therefore the representatives of the United States of America in General Congress assembled, do, in the name & by authority of the good people of these states, reject & renounce all allegiance & subjection to the kings of Great Britain & all others who may hereafter claim by, through, or under them; we utterly dissolve all political connection which may have heretofore subsisted between us & the people or parliament of Great Britain; and finally we do assert and declare these colonies to be free and independant states, and that as free & independant states they shall hereafter have full power to levy war, conclude peace, contract alliances, establish commerce, & to do all other acts and things which independant states may of right do. And for the support of this declaration we mutually pledge to each other our lives, our fortunes, & our sacred honour.

DOCUMENT V. *Jefferson's Rough Draft, page four*

Copy of the Declaration Made by Jefferson for Richard Henry Lee

Reproduced from photographs of the original in the American Philosophical Society, supplied through the courtesy of Dr. Edward G. Conklin, President of the Society. This copy was sent by Jefferson to Lee on July 8, 1776, who explained that it was "as originally framed," by which he must have meant as originally reported by the Committee of Five to Congress, for it approximates the state of the Declaration as it was when the Committee finished its deliberations. It was presented to the American Philosophical Society in 1825 by Lee's grandson. Correspondence between Jefferson and John Vaughan, together with other documents and a slightly reduced facsimile of the Lee copy, is published in a scholarly account of its history by I. Minis Hays in *Proceedings of the American Philosophical Society*, XXXVII (1898), p. 88–107. *See also,* Hazelton, *op. cit.,* p. 344–46.

Courtesy of the American Philosophical Society, Philadelphia.

a Declaration by the Representatives of the UNITED STATES OF AMERICA in General Congress assembled.

When in the course of human events it becomes necessary for one people to dissolve the political bands which have connected them with another, and to assume among the powers of the earth the separate and equal station to which the laws of nature and of nature's god entitle them, a decent respect to the opinions of mankind requires that they should declare the causes which impel them to the separation.

We hold these truths to be self-evident; that all men are created equal; that

sustain un-
alienable rights

they are endowed by their Creator with inherent and inalienable rights; that among these are life, liberty, and the pursuit of happiness; that to secure these rights, governments are instituted among men, deriving their just powers from the consent of the governed; that whenever any form of government becomes destructive of these ends, it is the right of the people to alter or to abolish it, and to institute new government, laying it's foundation on such principles, and organising it's powers in such form as to them shall seem most likely to effect their safety and happiness. prudence indeed will dictate that governments long established should not be changed for light & trans-

& alter

ient causes. and accordingly all experience hath shewn, that mankind are more disposed to suffer, while evils are sufferable than to right themselves by abolishing the forms to which they are accustomed. but when a long train of abuses and usurpations, begun at a distin-

left out

guished period & pursuing invariably the same object evinces a design to reduce them under absolute despotism, it is their right, it is their duty, to throw off such government, & to provide new guards for their future security. such has been the patient sufferance of these

alter

colonies, & such is now the necessity which constrains them to expunge their former systems

repeated

of government. the history of the present king of Great Britain, is a history of unremitting

left out

injuries and usurpations, among which appears no solitary fact to contradict the

having

uniform tenor of the rest; but all have in direct object the establishment of an absolute tyranny over these states. to prove this let facts be submitted to a candid world, for

left out

the truth of which we pledge a faith yet unsullied by falsehood.

He has refused his assent to laws the most wholesome and necessary for the public good.
he has forbidden his governors to pass laws of immediate & pressing importance, unless suspended in their operation till his assent should be obtained; and when so suspended, he has neglected utterly to attend to them.

utterly ne-
glected

he has refused to pass other laws for the accomodation of large districts of people, unless those people would relinquish the right of representation in the legislature; a right inestimable to them, & formidable to tyrants only.

DOCUMENT VI. *Copy made by Jefferson for Richard Henry Lee, page one* he has called together legislative bodies at places unusual, uncomfortable, & distant from the depository of their public records, for the sole purpose of fatiguing them into compliance with his measures.

he has dissolved Representative houses repeatedly & continually, for opposing with manly firmness his invasions on the rights of the people.

he has refused for a long time after such dissolutions to cause others to be elected whereby the legislative powers, incapable of annihilation, have returned to the people at large for their exercise, the state remaining in the mean time exposed to all the dangers of invasion from without, & convulsions within.

he has endeavored to prevent the population of these states; for that purpose obstructing the laws for naturalization of foreigners; refusing to pass others to encourage their migrations hither; & raising the conditions of new appropriations of lands.

he has suffered the administration of justice totally to cease in some of these states, refusing his assent to laws for establishing judiciary powers.

he has made our judges dependant on his will alone, for the tenure of their offices, and the amount & paiment of their salaries.

he has erected a multitude of new offices by a self-assumed power, & sent hither swarms of officers to harrass our people, and eat out their substance.

he has kept among us, in times of peace, standing armies and ships of war, without the consent of our legislatures.

he has affected to render the military independant of, & superior to, the civil power.

he has combined with others to subject us to a jurisdiction foreign to our constitutions and unacknoleged by our laws; giving his assent to their acts of pretended legislation

for quartering large bodies of armed troops among us;

for protecting them by a mock-trial from punishment for any murders which they should commit on the inhabitants of these states;

for cutting off our trade with all parts of the world;

for imposing taxes on us without our consent;

for depriving us of the benefits of trial by jury;

for transporting us beyond seas to be tried for pretended offences;

for abolishing the free system of English laws in a neighboring province, establishing therein an arbitrary government, and enlarging it's boundaries so as to render it at once an example & fit instrument for introducing the same absolute rule into these states;

for taking away our charters, abolishing our most valuable laws, and altering fundamentally the forms of our governments;

DOCUMENT VI. *Copy made by Jefferson for Richard Henry Lee, page two*

for suspending our own legislatures & declaring themselves invested with power to
legislate for us in all cases whatsoever.

he has abdicated government here, withdrawing his governors, & declaring us out of his allegiance and protection, & waging war against us.

he has plundered our seas, ravaged our coasts, burnt our towns & destroyed the lives of our people
...
desolation & tyranny already begun with circumstances of cruelty & perfidy unworthy the head
of a civilized nation.

he has endeavored to bring on the inhabitants of our frontiers, the merciless Indian savages whose
known rule of warfare is an undistinguished destruction of all ages, sexes, & conditions of existence.
... with the allurements of forfeiture & confiscation of our property.

he has constrained ... the high seas to bear arms against their ...

he has waged cruel war against human nature itself, violating it's most sacred rights of
life & liberty in the persons of a distant people who never offended him, captivating
and carrying them into slavery in another hemisphere, or to incur miserable death
in their transportation thither. this piratical warfare, the opprobrium of infidel
powers, is the warfare of the Christian king of Great Britain. determined to keep
open a market where MEN should be bought & sold, he has prostituted his negative
for suppressing every legislative attempt to prohibit or to restrain this execrable commerce.
... he is now exciting those very people to rise in arms among us, and to purchase that liberty of which he has deprived them, by murdering the people upon whom he also obtruded them: thus paying off former crimes committed against the liberties of one
people with crimes which he urges them to commit against the lives of another.

... terms, our repeated petitions ... answered only by repeated injury. a prince
whose character is thus marked by every act which may define a tyrant, is unfit to be
the ruler of a people who mean to be free.

... in the short compass of twelve years only ... to build
a foundation so broad and undisguised for tyranny over a people fostered and
fixed in principles of freedom.

DOCUMENT VI. *Copy made by Jefferson for Richard Henry Lee, page three*

Nor have we been wanting in attentions to our British brethren. we have warned them from time to time of attempts by their legislature to extend a jurisdiction over these our states. we have reminded them of the circumstances of our emigration and settlement here, no one of which could warrant so strange a pretension: that these were effected at the expense of our own blood and treasure, unassisted by the wealth or the strength of ...

... one common ... for ... league and amity with them ... as part of our constitution nor ... of history may be ... appealed to their native justice & magnanimity, as well as to ... disavow these usurpations, which were likely to interrupt our connection ... experience. they too have ... occasions have been given ...

... chief magistrate ... over not only soldiers of our common blood but Scotch and foreign mercenaries to invade and destroy us. these facts have given the last stab to agonizing affection; and manly spirit bids us to renounce for ... these unfeeling brethren, we must endeavour to forget ... hold them as we hold the rest of mankind, enemies in war, in peace friends. we might have been a free & a great people together; but a communication of grandeur & of freedom it seems is below their dignity ... the road to happiness and to glory ... the ... which denounces our eternal separation!

We therefore the Representatives of the United States of America in General Congress assembled, do ... authority of the good people of these states ... and renounce all allegiance and subjection to ... Great Britain & all others who may hereafter claim by, through or under ... utterly dissolve all political connection which may ... parliament or people ...

... states & that as free & independant states they have full power to levy war, conclude peace, contract alliances, establish commerce, & to do all other acts and things which independant states may of right do. and for the support of this declaration we mutually pledge to each other our lives, our fortunes, and our sacred honor.

DOCUMENT VI. *Copy made by Jefferson for Richard Henry Lee, page four*

Unidentified Copy of the Declaration Made by Jefferson
[Cassius F. Lee Copy]

Reproduced from the original through the courtesy of the President and Board of Trustees of the New York Public Library, who also consented to place it on exhibit in the current <1943> Jefferson exhibit at the Library of Congress. This copy was purchased for the New York Public Library in 1896 from Dr. Thomas Addis Emmet, who in turn secured it from Eliot Danforth. The latter purchased it from Cassius F. Lee of Alexandria, Virginia. Since its early history is hidden in obscurity, the person for whom Jefferson made it is not known. In addition to the copy made for Richard Henry Lee, Jefferson sent other copies, which evidently were made between July 4 and July 10, to George Wythe, John Page, Edmund Pendleton, and Philip Mazzei. The present copy may be one of these, but this fact has not been positively established. See Hazelton, *op. cit.*, p. 347–48. This copy corresponds closely to the Lee copy in respect to its contents: that is, it represents the Declaration approximately as it was when the Committee of Five reported it to Congress.

Thomas Addis Emmet Collection, Manuscripts and Archives Division, The New York Public Library, Astor, Lenox and Tilden Foundations.

Note on the Copy Sent by Jefferson to George Wythe

John H. Hazelton, in his invaluable pioneering study on the Declaration of Independence, quoted (p. 350) the *Richmond* (Virginia) *Enquirer* of August 6, 1822, as saying it had "published … about thirteen years ago a copy of the original draft [of the Declaration] as it came from his [Jefferson's] own hands. This copy … was found among the papers of Mr. Wythe, the friend and instructor of his early years. This copy was published in Niles's W<eekly> Register, & in various other newspapers of this continent." Hazelton (p. 602) was unable to locate it as published in the *Richmond Enquirer* and elsewhere about 1809. In consequence, there has been doubt as to whether the copy in the New York Public Library (Document VII) or that in the Massachusetts Historical Society (Document IX) could be the Wythe copy. For the reasons given <here> it is believed that the copy in the New York Public Library is, in all probability, the copy sent to Wythe.

    Among the Jefferson Papers in the Library of Congress there is a box of newspaper clippings, one of which is taken from *The Commonwealth* (Pittsburgh, Pennsylvania) for July 1, 1807.

This clipping is endorsed in Jefferson's hand: "Declaration of Independence" and the printing of the Declaration is prefaced by the following comment of *The Commonwealth:* "We have chosen to publish, at this time the original draught of the Declaration of Independence, as it came from the pen of Mr. Jefferson, found among the papers of the venerable George Wythe, after his decease, in the handwriting of the author. It will be seen, by a comparison with the Declaration, as adopted, that hardly any instrument of writing, of the same length, written by an individual, ever underwent fewer alterations and amendments, when submitted to an assembly for revision and adoption. It is evident, therefore, that Mr. Jefferson, at that time, expressed the sense of the nation at large—as he has ever since done—and, as we trust, he ever will do. The passages omitted in the original composition are printed in Italics." The italicized portions in *The Commentator <The Commonwealth>* agree almost precisely with the corresponding underlined passages in the New York Public Library copy, and in one particular especially: in the Wythe copy "General" is omitted from the title of the Declaration and in the latter it is marked for omission. This occurs in no other copy except that made for Madison (and, of course, in the copy in *Notes* from which the Madison copy was made). In addition to this circumstantial evidence, it should be noted that the New York Public Library copy was acquired from Cassius F. Lee—who also possessed the two later drafts of Jefferson's ideas on a constitution for Virginia. Jefferson's proposed constitution was sent to Williamsburg by George Wythe. Could it be that the two drafts that belonged to Cassius F. Lee were those actually carried by Wythe? One of these drafts lacks the part that formed the Preamble to the Virginia Constitution: could it be that Wythe detached that part and presented it to the Virginia Convention? These, of course, are purely speculative questions, but the presence in Cassius F. Lee's hands of a copy of the Declaration bearing such exact relationship with the Wythe copy as printed in *The Commentator <Commonwealth>,* together with his possession of two drafts of a document which Wythe transmitted for Jefferson, lends strong color of probability to the supposition that the New York Public Library copy is the George Wythe copy. The point is not conclusively established and so, in these pages, the copy in the New York Public Library is referred to as the Cassius F. Lee copy.

A Declaration by the Representatives of the UNITED STATES OF AMERICA in General Congress assembled.

When in the course of human events it becomes necessary for one people to dissolve the political bands which have connected them with another, and to assume among the powers of the earth the separate and equal station to which the laws of nature & of nature's god entitle them, a decent respect to the opinions of mankind requires that they should declare the causes which impel them to the separation.

We hold these truths to be self-evident; that all men are created equal; that they are endowed by their Creator with inherent & inalienable rights; that among these are life, liberty, & the pursuit of happiness; that to secure these rights governments are instituted among men, deriving their just powers from the consent of the governed; that whenever any form of government becomes destructive of these ends, it is the right of the people to alter or to abolish it, and to institute new government, laying it's foundation on such principles & organising it's powers in such form as to them shall seem most likely to effect their safety & happiness. prudence indeed will dictate that governments long established should not be changed for light & transient causes. and accordingly all experience hath shewn that mankind are more disposed to suffer while evils are sufferable, ———————, themselves by abolishing the forms they are accustomed. but when a long train of abuses & usurpations, begun at a distinguished period, & pursuing invariably the same object, evinces a design to reduce them under absolute despotism, it is their right, it is their duty, to throw off such government & to provide new guards for their future security. such has been the patient sufferance of these colonies; & such is now the necessity which constrains them to expunge their former systems of government. the history of the present king of Great Britain, is a history of unremitting injuries & usurpations, among which appears no solitary fact to contradict the uniform tenor of the rest; but all have in direct object the establishment of an absolute tyranny over these states. to prove this let facts be submitted to a candid world, for the truth of which we pledge a faith yet unsullied by falsehood

he has refused his assent to laws the most wholesome & necessary for the public good:

he has forbidden his governors to pass laws of immediate & pressing importance, unless suspended in their operation till his assent should be obtained; & when so suspended, he has neglected utterly to attend to them:

he has refused to pass other laws for the accommodation of large districts of people, unless those people would relinquish the right of representation in the legislature, a right inestimable to them & formidable to tyrants only:

DOCUMENT VII. *Copy made by Jefferson [Cassius F. Lee copy], page one*

he has called together legislative bodies at places unusual uncomfortable, & distant
from the depository of their public records, for the sole purpose of fatiguing them
into compliance with his measures:

he has dissolved Representative houses repeatedly & continually for opposing with
manly firmness his invasions on the rights of the people:

he has refused for a long time after such dissolutions to cause others to be elected, whereby the legislative powers, incapable of annihilation, have returned to the people
at large for their exercise, the state remaining in the mean time exposed to all the
dangers of invasion from without, & convulsions within:

he has endeavored to prevent the population of these states; for that purpose obstructing
the laws for naturalization of foreigners, refusing to pass others to encourage their
migrations hither; & raising the conditions of new appropriations of lands:

he has suffered the administration of justice totally to cease in some of these states, refusing
his assent to laws for establishing judiciary powers:

he has made our judges dependant on his will alone, for the tenure of their offices & the
amount & paiment of their salaries:

he has erected a multitude of new offices by a self assumed power, & sent hither swarms
of officers to harrass our people & eat _____

he has kept among us in times of peace standing armies & ships of war, without the consent of our legislatures:

he has affected to render the military independant of, and superior to, the civil power:

he has combined with others to subject us to a jurisdiction foreign to our constitutions, and
unacknoleged by our laws; giving his assent to their acts of pretended legislation

for quartering large bodies of armed troops among us;

for protecting them by a mock-trial from punishment for any murders which they
should commit on the inhabitants of these states;

for cutting off our trade with all parts of the world;

for imposing taxes on us without our consent;

for depriving us of the benefits of trial by jury;

for transporting us beyond seas to be tried for pretended offences;

for abolishing the free system of English laws in a neighboring province, establishing therein an arbitrary government, and enlarging it's boundaries, so as to
render it at once an example & fit instrument for introducing the same absolute rule into these states;

for taking away our charters, abolishing our most valuable laws, and altering

DOCUMENT VII. *Copy made by Jefferson [Cassius F. Lee copy], page two* fundamentally the forms of our governments;

for suspending our own legislatures & declaring themselves invested with power to legislate for us in all cases whatsoever:

he has abdicated government here, withdrawing his governors, & declaring us out of his allegiance & protection:

he has plundered our seas, ravaged our coasts, burnt our towns, & destroyed the lives of our people:

he is at this time transporting large armies of foreign mercenaries to compleat the works of death, desolation & tyranny, already begun with circumstances of cruelty & perfidy unworthy the head of a civilized nation:

he has endeavored to bring on the inhabitants of our frontiers the merciless Indian savages, whose known rule of warfare is an undistinguished destruction of all ages, sexes, & conditions of existence:

he has incited treasonable insurrections of our fellow-citizens, with the allurements of forfeiture & confiscation of our property:

he has constrained others, taken captives on the high seas, to bear arms against their country, to become the executioners of their friends and brethren, or to fall themselves by their hands:

he has waged cruel war against human nature itself, violating it's most sacred rights of life & liberty in the persons of a distant people, who never offended him, captivating & carrying them into slavery in another hemisphere, or to incur miserable death in their transportation thither. this piratical warfare, the opprobrium of infidel powers, is the warfare of the Christian king of Great Britain. determined to keep open a market where MEN should be bought & sold, he has prostituted his negative for suppressing every legislative attempt to prohibit or to restrain this execrable commerce: and that this assemblage of horrors might want no fact of distinguished dye, he is now exciting those very people to rise in arms among us, and to purchase that liberty of which he has deprived them by murdering the people upon whom he also obtruded them; thus paying off former crimes committed against the liberties of one people, with crimes which he urges them to commit against the lives of another.

in every stage of these oppressions, we have petitioned for redress in the most humble terms; our repeated petitions have been answered only by repeated injury. a prince whose character is thus marked by every act which may define a tyrant, is unfit to be the ruler of a people who mean to be free. future ages will scarce believe that the hardiness of one man adventured within the short compass of twelve years only, to build a foundation, so broad & undisguised for tyranny over a people fostered & fixed in principles of freedom.

DOCUMENT VII. *Copy made by Jefferson [Cassius F. Lee copy], page three*

Nor have we been wanting in attentions to our British brethren. we have warned them from time to time of attempts by their legislature to extend a jurisdiction over these our states. we have reminded them of the circumstances of our emigration & settlement here, no one of which could warrant so strange a pretension: that these were effected at the expence of our own blood & treasure, unassisted by the wealth or the strength of Great Britain: that in constituting indeed our several forms of government, we had a-dopted one common king, thereby laying a foundation for perpetual league & amity with them: but that submission to their parliament was no part of our constitution, nor ever in idea, if history may be credited: and we appealed to their native justice & magnanimity, as well as to the ties of our common kindred, to disavow these usur-pations, which were likely to interrupt our connection & correspondence. they too have been deaf to the voice of justice & of consanguinity, and when occasions have been given them, by the regular course of their laws, of removing from their councils the disturbers of our harmony, they have by their free election re-established them in power. at this very time too, they are permitting their chief magistrate to send over not only soldiers of our common blood, but [Scotch and] foreign mercenaries to invade & destroy us. these facts have given the last stab to agonizing affection and manly spirit bids us to renounce these unfeeling brethren. we must endeavor to forget our former love for them and to hold them, as we hold the rest of mankind, enemies in war, in peace friends. we might have been a free & a great people together; but a communication of grandeur and of freedom, it seems, is below their dignity. be it so, since they will have it: the road to happiness and to glory is open to us too; we will climb it apart from them, and ac-quiesce in the necessity which denounces our eternal separation!

We therefore the Representatives of the United states of America, in General Congress assembled, do, in the name & by authority of the good people of these states, reject and renounce all allegiance & subjection to the kings of Great Britain, and all others who may hereafter claim by, through, or under them; we utterly dissolve all political connection which may heretofore have subsisted between us & the parliament or people of Great Britain; and finally we do assert these colonies to be free & independent states, and that as free & independant states, they have full power to levy war, conclude peace, contract alliances, establish commerce, & to do all other acts and things which inde-pendant states may of right do. And for the support of this declaration, we mu-tually pledge to each other our lives, our fortunes & our sacred honor.

DOCUMENT VII. *Copy made by Jefferson [Cassius F. Lee copy], page four*

Copy of the Declaration Made by Jefferson for James Madison

Reproduced in actual size <in the 1943 edition>, from the original in the Madison Papers in the Library of Congress. This copy was made by Jefferson for Madison in the spring of 1783 and enclosed in a letter to Madison dated June 1, 1783. It was made from Jefferson's *Notes* which he put into form some time after July 4, 1776, and before June 1, 1783. The *Notes,* being in narrative form, were in turn based on notes taken during the debates. The original manuscript of the *Notes* was inserted in 1821 by Jefferson in his Autobiography. The Madison copy, rather than the version in the *Notes,* has been reproduced here because of the particular point involved in the crossed out phrases at the top of page 8 of the Madison copy. The pages of the Madison copy were apparently joined in book form at one time, but are now mounted as separate leaves <in a bound volume>. They should be read, therefore, as if the left and right pages at top and bottom were joined at the center. The Madison copy is given in full so far as it relates to the text of the Declaration, together with a portion of the debate in Congress on its adoption. *See Writings of Jefferson,* P. L. Ford, ed., I, p. 28*ff.*

Papers of James Madison, Manuscript Division, Library of Congress.

Congress proceeded the same day to consider the declaration of Independance, which had been reported & laid on the table the Friday preceding, and on Monday referred to a commee of the whole. the pusillanimous idea that we had friends in England worth keeping terms with still haunted the minds of many. for this reason those passages which conveyed censures on the people of England were struck out lest they should give them offence. the clause too reprobating the enslaving the inhabitants of Africa was struck out in complaisance to S. Carolina & Georgia, who had never attempted to restrain the importation of slaves, & who on the contrary still wished to continue it. our Northern brethren also I believe, felt a little tender under those censures; for tho' their people have very few slaves themselves, yet they had been pretty considerable carriers of them to others. the debates having taken up the greater parts of the 2d. 3d. & 4th. days of July, were, in the evening of the last, closed; the decla-

8

-ration was reported by the commee, agreed to by the house, & signed by every member except mr Dickinson. as the sentiments of men are known not only by what they receive, but what they reject also, I will state the form of the declaration as origi-nally reported. the parts struck out by Congress shall be distinguished by a black line drawn under them, & those inserted by them shall be placed in the margin or in a concurrent column.

A Declaration by the representatives of the United States of America in [General] Congress assembled.

When in the course of human events it becomes necessary for one people to dis-solve the political bands which have con-nected them with another, & to assume among the powers of the earth the separate & equal station to which the laws of nature & nature's god entitle them, a decent respect to the opinions of mankind requires that they should declare the causes which impel them to the separation.

We hold these truths to be self-evident: that all men are created equal; that they are endowed by their creator with [inherent &] inalienable rights; that among these are life, liberty & the pursuit of happiness; that to secure these rights, governments are instituted among men, deriving their just powers from the consent of the governed; that whenever any form of government becomes destruc-tive of these ends, it is the right of the people to alter or to abolish it, & to institute new government lay-ing it's foundation on such principles & organising it's powers in such form, as to them shall seem most likely to effect their safety & happiness. prudence indeed will dictate that governments long established should not be changed for light & transient causes; and accordingly all experi-ence hath shewn that mankind are more disposed to suffer while evils

certain

9

are sufferable, than to right themselves by abolishing the forms to which they are accustomed. but when a long train of abuses & usurpations [begun at a distin-guished period and] pursuing invari-ably the same object, evinces a design to reduce them under absolute despo-tism, it is their right, it is their duty to throw off such government, & to provide new guards for their future security. such has been the patient sufferance of these colonies, & such is now the necessity which constrains them to [expunge] their for-mer systems of government. the history of the present king of Great Britain is a history of [unremitting] injuries & usur-pations [among which appears no solitary fact to contradict the uniform tenor of the rest, but all have] in direct object the establishment of an absolute tyranny over these states. to prove this let facts be submitted to a candid world [for the truth of which we pledge a faith yet un-sullied by falsehood]

alter

repeated

all having

DOCUMENT VIII. *Copy made by Jefferson for James Madison, pages one to four* he has refused his assent to laws the most wholesome & necessary for the public good.

he has forbidden his governors to pass laws of immediate & pressing importance, unless suspended in their operation till his assent should be obtained; & when so suspended he has utterly neglected to attend to them.

he has refused to pass other laws for the accomodation of large districts of people, unless those people would relinquish the right of representation in the legislature a right inestimable to them, & formidable to tyrants only.

he has called together legislative bodies at places unusual, uncomfortable & distant from the depository of their public records, for the sole purpose of fatiguing them into compliance with his measures

he has dissolved representative houses repeatedly [and continually] for opposing with manly firmness his invasions on the rights of the people.

he has refused for a long time after such dissolutions to cause others to be elected, whereby the legislative powers, incapable of annihilation, have returned to the people at large for their exercise, the state remaining in the mean time exposed to all the dangers of invasion from without & convulsions within.

he has endeavored to prevent the population of these states; for that purpose obstructing the laws for naturalization of foreigners, refusing to pass others to encourage their migrations hither, & raising the conditions of new appropriations of land.

he has [suffered] the administration of justice [totally] to cease in some of these states, refusing his assent to laws *Obstructed* *by*

for establishing judiciary powers.

he has made [our] judges dependent on his will alone for the tenure of their offices & the amount & paiment of their salaries.

he has erected a multitude of new offices [by a selfassumed power] and sent hither swarms of new officers to harrass our people & eat out their substance

he has kept among us in times of peace standing armies [& ships of war] without the consent of our legislatures.

he has affected to render the military independant of & superior to the civil power.

he has combined with others to subject us to a jurisdiction foreign to our constitutions & unacknoleged by our laws, giving his assent to their acts of pretended legislation for quartering large bodies of armed troops among us; for protecting them by a mock trial from punishment for any murders which they should commit on the inhabitants of these

states; for cutting off our trade with all parts of the world; for imposing taxes on us without our consent; for depriving us of the benefits of trial by jury; for transporting us beyond seas to be tried for pretended offences; for abolishing the free system of English laws in a neighboring province, establishing therein an arbitrary government, & enlarging it's boundaries, so as to render it at once an example & fit instrument for introducing the same absolute rule into these [states]; for taking away our charters, abolishing our most valuable laws, & altering fundamentally the forms of our governments; for suspending our own legislatures & declaring themselves invested with power to legislate for us in all cases whatsoever. *in many cases* *colonies*

he has abdicated government here

DOCUMENT VIII. *Copy made by Jefferson for James Madison, pages five to eight*

[Withdrawing his governors & declaring us out of his allegiance & protection]

by declaring us out of his protection & waging war against us

he has plundered our seas, ravaged our coasts, burnt our towns, & destroyed the lives of our people.

he is at this time transporting large armies of foreign mercenaries to compleat the works of death, desolation & tyranny already begun with circumstances of cruelty & perfidy, unworthy the head of a civilized nation.

scarcely paralleled in the most barbarous ages, & totally

he has constrained our fellow citizens taken captive on the high seas to bear arms against their country, to become the executioners of their friends & brethren, or to fall themselves by their hands.

excited domestic insurrections among us & has

he has endeavored to bring on the inhabitants of our frontiers the merciless Indian savages whose known rule of warfare is an undistinguished destruction of all ages, sexes & conditions [of existence.]

[he has incited treasonable insurrections of our fellow-citizens with the allurements of forfeiture & confiscation of our property.]

he has waged cruel war against human nature itself, violating it's

12

---

most sacred rights of life & liberty in the persons of a distant people who never offended him, captivating & carrying them into slavery in another hemisphere, or to incur miserable death in their transportation thither. this piratical warfare, the opprobrium of infidel powers, is the warfare of the Christian king of Great Britain. determined to keep open a market where Men should be bought & sold, he has prostituted his negative for suppressing every legislative attempt to prohibit or to restrain this execrable commerce. and that this assemblage of horrors might want no fact of distinguished die he is now exciting those very people to rise in arms among us, and to purchase that liberty of which he has deprived them by murdering the people on whom he also obtruded them: thus paying off former crimes committed against the liberties of one people, with crimes which he urges them to commit against the lives of another.

In every stage of these oppressions we have petitioned for redress in the most humble terms. our repeated petitions have been answered only by repeated injuries. a prince whose character is thus marked by every act which may define a tyrant, is unfit to be the ruler of a people [who mean to be free.

free

future ages will scarcely believe that the hardiness of one man adventured within the short compass of twelve years only, to lay a foundation so broad & so undisguised for tyranny over a people fostered & fixed in principles of freedom.]

Nor have we been wanting in attentions to our British brethren. we have warned them from time to time of attempts by their legislature to extend [a] jurisdiction over

an unwarrantable
us.

[these our states.] we have reminded them of the circumstances of our emigration & settlement here [no one of which could warrant so strange a pretension. that these were effected at the expence of our own blood & treasure, unassisted by the wealth or the strength of Great Britain: that in constituting indeed our several forms of

13

---

government, we had adopted one common king, thereby laying a foundation for perpetual league & amity with them: but that submission to their parliament was no part of our constitution, nor ever in idea, if history may be credited: and] we appealed to their native justice and magnanimity, [as well as to] the ties of our common kindred to disavow these usurpations which [were likely to] interrupt our connection and correspondence.

have
and we have conjured them by
would inevitably

they too have been deaf to the voice of justice & of consanguinity. [and when occasions have been given them by the regular course of their laws, of removing from their councils the disturbers of our harmony, they have by their free election re-established them in power. at this very time too they are permitting their chief magistrate to send over not only soldiers of our common blood but Scotch & foreign mercenaries to invade & destroy us. these facts have given the last stab to agonizing affection, and manly spirit bids us to renounce

DOCUMENT VIII. *Copy made by Jefferson for James Madison, pages nine to twelve*

for ever these unfeeling brethren. we must
endeavor to forget our former love for them,
and to hold them as we hold the rest of man
-kind, enemies in war, in peace friends.
we might have been a free & a great peo
-ple together; but a communication of
grandeur & of freedom it seems is below
their dignity. be it so, since they will
have it. the road to happiness & to
glory is open to us too. we will tread it
apart from them, and, acquiesce in
the necessity which denounces our [eter
-nal] separation!

We therefore the representatives of the
United states of America in General Congress
assembled

appealing to the supreme judge	do in the name & by authority
of the world for the rectitude	of the good people of these states
of our intentions, do, in the	reject & renounce all allegiance
name & by the authority of	& subjection to the kings of great
the good people of these colo	Britain & all others who may
-nies solemnly publish &	hereafter claim by, through, or
declare that these United	under them: we utterly dis
colonies are & of right	-solve all political connec
ought to be free & independ	-tion which may heretofore
-ant states; that they are	have subsisted between us
absolved from all allegiance	& the people or parliament of

14

we must therefore to hold them as we hold the rest of mankind ene- mies in war, in peace friends.

to the British crown, & that
all political connection be
-tween them & the state
of great Britain is & ought
to be totally dissolved;
and that as free & independant states
they have full power to levy war, conclude
peace, contract alliances, establish com
-merce, & to do all other acts & things which
independant states may of right do. and
for the support of this declaration, we mu
-tually pledge to each other our lives, our
fortunes & our sacred honor.

Great Britain: & finally
we do assert & declare
these colonies to be free
& independant states

with a firm reliance on the protection of divine provi -dence

On Friday July 12. the committee
appointed to draw the articles of Confe
-deration reported them, & on the 22d
the house resolved themselves into a
committee to take them into considera
-tion. on the 30th & 31st of that month
& 1st of the ensuing, those articles were
debated which determined the propor
-tion or quota of money which each state
should furnish to the common treasury
& the manner of voting in Congress.

Unidentified Copy of the Declaration Made by Jefferson
[The Washburn Copy]

Reproduced from the original in the Massachusetts Historical Society, through the courtesy of the officers of that institution, who also consented to have it placed on exhibit in the current <1943> Jefferson exhibition at the Library of Congress. The provenance of this copy is not known beyond 1893 when Alexander C. Washburn and his wife presented it to the Massachusetts Historical Society. They probably secured it by purchase, but from whom is not known. It may possibly be one of the copies sent by Jefferson to Wythe, Pendleton, or Page. The second leaf has been mutilated, so that two-thirds of the text on pages three and four has been lost. The copy corresponds approximately to the state of the Richard Henry Lee copy as respects its text. The observant reader will notice on the first page of the reproduction the faint outlines of a man's portrait. This comes from a slight discoloration caused by its juxtaposition, in the volume in which it was mounted by the Washburns, to a lithograph done after the Stuart portrait of Jefferson.

Courtesy Massachusetts Historical Society, Boston.

A Declaration by the Representatives of the United States of America in General Congress assembled.

When in the course of human events it becomes necessary for one people to dissolve the political bands which have connected them with another, & to assume among the powers of the earth the separate & equal station, to which the laws of nature & of nature's god entitle them, a decent respect to the opinions of mankind requires that they should declare the causes which impel them to the separation.

We hold these truths to be self-evident: that all men are created equal: that they are endowed by their creator with inherent & inalienable rights: that among these are life, liberty & the pursuit of happiness: that to secure these rights, governments are instituted among men, deriving their just powers from the consent of the governed: that whenever any form of government becomes destructive of these ends, it is the right of the people to alter or to abolish it, & to institute new government, laying it's foundation on such principles, & organising it's powers in such form, as to them shall seem most likely to effect their safety and happiness. prudence indeed will dictate that governments long established should not be changed for light and transient causes: and accordingly all experience hath shewn that mankind are more disposed to suffer while evils are sufferable, than to right themselves by abolishing the forms to which they are accustomed. but when a long train of abuses & usurpations, begun at a distinguished period, & pursuing invariably the same object, evinces a design to reduce them under absolute despotism, it is their right, it is their duty, to throw off such government, & to provide new guards for their future security. such has been the patient sufferance of these colonies; and such is now the necessity which constrains them to expunge their former systems of government. the history of the present king of Great Britain is a history of unremitting injuries & usurpations, among which appears no solitary fact to contradict the uniform tenor of the rest, but all have in direct object the establishment of an absolute tyranny over these states. to prove this, let facts be submitted to a candid world, for the truth of which we pledge a faith yet unsullied by falsehood.

He has refused his assent to laws the most wholesome and necessary for the public good.

he has forbidden his governors to pass laws of immediate & pressing importance, unless suspended in their operation till his assent should be obtained; and when so suspended, he has neglected utterly to attend to them.

DOCUMENT IX. *Copy made by Jefferson [Washburn copy], page one*

he has refused to pass other laws for the accomodation of large districts of people, unless those people would relinquish the right of representation in the legislature, a right inestimable to them, & formidable to tyrants only.

he has called together legislative bodies at places unusual, uncomfortable, & distant from the depository of their public records, for the sole purpose of fatigueing them into compliance with his measures.

he has dissolved Representative houses repeatedly & continually, for opposing with manly firmness his invasions on the rights of the people.

he has refused for a long time after such dissolutions to cause others to be elected, whereby the legislative powers, incapable of annihilation, have returned to the people at large for their exercise, the state remaining in the mean time, exposed to all the dangers of invasion from without, & convulsions within.

he has endeavored to prevent the population of these states; for that purpose obstructing the laws for naturalization of foreigners; refusing to pass others to encourage their migrations hither; & raising the conditions of new appropriations of lands.

he has suffered the administration of justice totally to cease in some of these states, refusing his assent to laws for establishing judiciary powers

he has made our judges dependant on his will alone, for the tenure of their offices, & the amount & paiment of their salaries.

he has erected a multitude of new offices by a self-assumed power, & sent hither swarms of officers to harrass our people & eat out their substance.

he has kept among us, in times of peace, standing armies & ships of war without the consent of our legislatures.

he has affected to render the military independant of & superior to the civil power.

he has combined with others to subject us to a jurisdiction foreign to our constitutions and unacknoleged by our laws; giving his assent to their acts of pretended legislation for quartering large bodies of armed troops among us;

for protecting them by a mock trial from punishment for any murders which they should commit on the inhabitants of these states;

for cutting off our trade with all parts of the world;

for imposing taxes on us without our consent;

for depriving us of the benefits of trial by jury;

for transporting us beyond seas to be tried for pretended offences;

DOCUMENT IX. *Copy made by Jefferson [Washburn copy], page two* for abolishing the free system of English laws in a neighboring province, establishing therein an arbitrary government, & enlarging it's boundaries, so as to render it at once an example and fit instrument for introducing the same absolute rule into these states;

for taking away our charters, abolishing our most valuable laws, & altering fundamentally the forms of our governments;

for suspending our own legislatures & declaring themselves invested with power to legislate for us in all cases whatsoever.

he has abdicated government here, withdrawing his governors, & declaring us out of his

character is thus marked by every act which may define a tyrant, is unfit to be the ruler of a people who mean to be free. future ages will scarce believe that the hardiness of one man adventured within the short compass of twelve years only, to build a foundation, so broad & undisguised, for tyranny over a people fostered & fixed in principles of freedom.

Nor have we been wanting in attentions to our British brethren. we have warned them from time to time of attempts by their legislature to extend a jurisdiction over these our states. , we have reminded them of the circumstances of our emigration and settlement here, no one of which could warrant so strange a pretension: that these were effected at the expence of our own blood & treasure, unassisted by the wealth or the strength of Great Britain: that in constituting indeed our several forms of government, we had adopted one common king, thereby laying a founda

DOCUMENT IX. *Copy made by Jefferson [Washburn copy], page four*

The First Printing of the Declaration
As Inserted in the Rough Journal of Congress

Reproduced, at some reduction, from the original in the Papers of the Continental Congress in the Library of Congress <in 1943, but transferred to the National Archives in 1952>. The Declaration is copied out by hand in the Corrected Journal, with two slight omissions which appear in the Rough Journal copy, but, perhaps owing to the stress of the memorable day, Charles Thomson did not copy out the Declaration in the Rough Journal, which is done in his handwriting, but left a space which he later filled by attaching to that page the broadside of the Declaration printed, perhaps during the night of July 4-5, by John Dunlap of Philadelphia.

Papers of the Continental Congress, National Archives and Records Administration.

IN CONGRESS, JULY 4, 1776.

A DECLARATION

BY THE REPRESENTATIVES OF THE
UNITED STATES OF AMERICA,

IN GENERAL CONGRESS ASSEMBLED.

WHEN in the Course of human Events, it becomes neceſſary for one People to diſſolve the Political Bands which have connected them with another, and to aſſume among the Powers of the Earth, the ſeparate and equal Station to which the Laws of Nature and of Nature's God entitle them, a decent Reſpect to the Opinions of Mankind requires that they ſhould declare the cauſes which impel them to the Separation.

WE hold theſe Truths to be ſelf-evident, that all Men are created equal, that they are endowed by their Creator with certain unalienable Rights, that among theſe are Life, Liberty, and the Purſuit of Happineſs--That to ſecure theſe Rights, Governments are inſtituted among Men, deriving their juſt Powers from the Conſent of the Governed, that whenever any Form of Government becomes deſtructive of theſe Ends, it is the Right of the People to alter or to aboliſh it, and to inſtitute new Government, laying its Foundation on ſuch Principles, and organizing its Powers in ſuch Form, as to them ſhall ſeem moſt likely to effect their Safety and Happineſs. Prudence, indeed, will dictate that Governments long eſtabliſhed ſhould not be changed for light and tranſient Cauſes; and accordingly all Experience hath ſhewn, that Mankind are more diſpoſed to ſuffer, while Evils are ſufferable, than to right themſelves by aboliſhing the Forms to which they are accuſtomed. But when a long Train of Abuſes and Uſurpations, purſuing invariably the ſame Object, evinces a Deſign to reduce them under abſolute Deſpotiſm, it is their Right, it is their Duty, to throw off ſuch Government, and to provide new Guards for their future Security. Such has been the patient Sufferance of theſe Colonies; and ſuch is now the Neceſſity which conſtrains them to alter their former Syſtems of Government. The Hiſtory of the preſent King of Great-Britain is a Hiſtory of repeated Injuries and Uſurpations, all having in direct Object the Eſtabliſhment of an abſolute Tyranny over theſe States. To prove this, let Facts be ſubmitted to a candid World.

HE has refuſed his Aſſent to Laws, the moſt wholeſome and neceſſary for the public Good.

HE has forbidden his Governors to paſs Laws of immediate and preſſing Importance, unleſs ſuſpended in their Operation till his Aſſent ſhould be obtained; and when ſo ſuſpended, he has utterly neglected to attend to them.

HE has refuſed to paſs other Laws for the Accommodation of large Diſtricts of People, unleſs thoſe People would relinquiſh the Right of Repreſentation in the Legiſlature, a Right ineſtimable to them, and formidable to Tyrants only.

HE has called together Legiſlative Bodies at Places unuſual, uncomfortable, and diſtant from the Depoſitory of their public Records, for the ſole Purpoſe of fatiguing them into Compliance with his Meaſures.

HE has diſſolved Repreſentative Houſes repeatedly, for oppoſing with manly Firmneſs his Invaſions on the Rights of the People.

HE has refuſed for a long Time, after ſuch Diſſolutions, to cauſe others to be elected; whereby the Legiſlative Powers, incapable of Annihilation, have returned to the People at large for their exerciſe; the State remaining in the mean time expoſed to all the Dangers of Invaſion from without, and Convulſions within.

HE has endeavoured to prevent the Population of theſe States; for that Purpoſe obſtructing the Laws for Naturalization of Foreigners; refuſing to paſs others to encourage their Migrations hither, and raiſing the Conditions of new Appropriations of Lands.

HE has obſtructed the Adminiſtration of Juſtice, by refuſing his Aſſent to Laws for eſtabliſhing Judiciary Powers.

HE has made Judges dependent on his Will alone, for the Tenure of their Offices, and the Amount and Payment of their Salaries.

HE has erected a Multitude of new Offices, and ſent hither Swarms of Officers to harraſs our People, and eat out their Subſtance.

HE has kept among us, in Times of Peace, Standing Armies, without the conſent of our Legiſlatures.

HE has affected to render the Military independent of and ſuperior to the Civil Power.

HE has combined with others to ſubject us to a Juriſdiction foreign to our Conſtitution, and unacknowledged by our Laws; giving his Aſſent to their Acts of pretended Legiſlation:

FOR quartering large Bodies of Armed Troops among us:

FOR protecting them, by a mock Trial, from Puniſhment for any Murders which they ſhould commit on the Inhabitants of theſe States:

FOR cutting off our Trade with all Parts of the World:

FOR impoſing Taxes on us without our Conſent:

FOR depriving us, in many Caſes, of the Benefits of Trial by Jury:

FOR tranſporting us beyond Seas to be tried for pretended Offences:

FOR aboliſhing the free Syſtem of Engliſh Laws in a neighbouring Province, eſtabliſhing therein an arbitrary Government, and enlarging its Boundaries, ſo as to render it at once an Example and fit Inſtrument for introducing the ſame abſolute Rule into theſe Colonies:

FOR taking away our Charters, aboliſhing our moſt valuable Laws, and altering fundamentally the Forms of our Governments:

FOR ſuſpending our own Legiſlatures, and declaring themſelves inveſted with Power to legiſlate for us in all Caſes whatſoever.

HE has abdicated Government here, by declaring us out of his Protection and waging War againſt us.

HE has plundered our Seas, ravaged our Coaſts, burnt our Towns, and deſtroyed the Lives of our People.

HE is, at this Time, tranſporting large Armies of foreign Mercenaries to compleat the Works of Death, Deſolation, and Tyranny, already begun with circumſtances of Cruelty and Perfidy, ſcarcely parallelled in the moſt barbarous Ages, and totally unworthy the Head of a civilized Nation.

HE has conſtrained our fellow Citizens taken Captive on the high Seas to bear Arms againſt their Country, to become the Executioners of their Friends and Brethren, or to fall themſelves by their Hands.

HE has excited domeſtic Inſurrections amongſt us, and has endeavoured to bring on the Inhabitants of our Frontiers, the mercileſs Indian Savages, whoſe known Rule of Warfare, is an undiſtinguiſhed Deſtruction, of all Ages, Sexes and Conditions.

IN every ſtage of theſe Oppreſſions we have Petitioned for Redreſs in the moſt humble Terms: Our repeated Petitions have been anſwered only by repeated Injury. A Prince, whoſe Character is thus marked by every act which may define a Tyrant, is unfit to be the Ruler of a free People.

NOR have we been wanting in Attentions to our Britiſh Brethren. We have warned them from Time to Time of Attempts by their Legiſlature to extend an unwarrantable Juriſdiction over us. We have reminded them of the Circumſtances of our Emigration and Settlement here. We have appealed to their native Juſtice and Magnanimity, and we have conjured them by the Ties of our common Kindred to diſavow theſe Uſurpations, which, would inevitably interrupt our Connections and Correſpondence. They too have been deaf to the Voice of Juſtice and of Conſanguinity. We muſt, therefore, acquieſce in the Neceſſity, which denounces our Separation, and hold them, as we hold the reſt of Mankind, Enemies in War, in Peace, Friends.

WE, therefore, the Repreſentatives of the UNITED STATES OF AMERICA, in GENERAL CONGRESS, Aſſembled, appealing to the Supreme Judge of the World for the Rectitude of our Intentions, do, in the Name, and by Authority of the good People of theſe Colonies, ſolemnly Publiſh and Declare, That theſe United Colonies are, and of Right ought to be, FREE AND INDEPENDENT STATES; that they are abſolved from all Allegiance to the Britiſh Crown, and that all political Connection between them and the State of Great-Britain, is and ought to be totally diſſolved; and that as FREE AND INDEPENDENT STATES, they have full Power to levy War, conclude Peace, contract Alliances, eſtabliſh Commerce, and to do all other Acts and Things which INDEPENDENT STATES may of right do. And for the ſupport of this Declaration, with a firm Reliance on the Protection of divine Providence, we mutually pledge to each other our Lives, our Fortunes, and our ſacred Honor.

Signed by ORDER _and in_ BEHALF _of the_ CONGRESS,

JOHN HANCOCK, PRESIDENT.

ATTEST.
CHARLES THOMSON, SECRETARY.

PHILADELPHIA: PRINTED BY JOHN DUNLAP.

DOCUMENT X. *The First Printing of the Declaration of Independence
Inserted in the Rough Journal of Congress*

Notes

1. In this brief analysis of the text of the various drafts of the Declaration I have leaned heavily upon Mr. Carl Becker's excellent study, *The Declaration of Independence: a Study in the History of Political Ideas* (2d ed., New York, 1942) and I wish to acknowledge an indebtedness which all readers of this book must feel and which in my case is very great. I have also found John H. Hazelton's *The Declaration of Independence* an indispensable source of information.

2. Marie Kimball, *Jefferson: the Road to Glory* (1943), p. 227–28.

3. Pickering made a very precise copy of the Richard Henry Lee copy at Washington on February 26, 1805 (now in the Massachusetts Historical Society), and doubtless his intention even at that date was the same as that stated in the above quotation, which was made in a letter to Henry Lee, May 3, 1811; Hazelton, *op. cit.,* p. 481–84.

4. *Letters of Members of the Continental Congress,* E. C. Burnett, ed., I, p. 515–16.

5. *Writings of Jefferson,* P. L. Ford, ed., X, p. 266. The letter is dated August 30, 1823.

6. *Ibid.,* VII, p. 407.

7. Charles F. Mullett, *Fundamental Law and the American Revolution,* p. 7.

8. Mr. Becker's work contains a masterly analysis of the natural rights philosophy and of the American view of the nature of the British constitution. See also Randolph G. Adams, *Political Ideas of the American Revolution* (Durham, 1922).

9. Mullett, *op. cit., passim.*

10. Marie Kimball, *op. cit.,* 103–106. The letter is dated July 17, 1771.

11. It should be noted that the instructions to the Virginia delegates in Congress included the word "Parliament," which therein differed from the Resolution of Independence offered by Richard Henry Lee on June 7. News of the Virginia action reached Philadelphia on May 27. Hugh Blair Grigsby, *The Virginia Convention of 1776,* p. 18*ff.*; Marie Kimball, *op. cit.,* p. 283–84.

12. *Works of John Adams,* C. F. Adams, ed., II, p. 510.

13. Burnett, *op. cit.,* p. 445; <and *Letters of Delegates to Congress, 1774–1789,* Paul H. Smith et al., eds., III, p. 429–32.> In a letter to Horatio Gates, March 23, 1776, Adams had expressed the thought that the Act of Parliament declaring the Colonies beyond the protection of the Crown—"the prohibitory Act, or piratical Act, or plundering Act, or Act of Independency"—was a complete dismemberment of the British Empire. "It may be fortunate," he added, "that the Act of Independency should come from the British Parliament, rather than the American Congress: But it is very odd that Americans should hesitate at accepting such a gift"; Hazelton, *op. cit.,* p. 95.

14. Duane to John Jay, May 11 and 16, 1776, Burnett, *op. cit.,* I, p. 443–44; <and *Letters of Delegates, op. cit.,* III, p. 652–53 (May 11) and IV, p. 5 (May 16)>; *Works of John Adams,* III, p. 46; Hazelton, *op. cit.,* p. 106–107.

15. Burnett, *op. cit.,* I, p. 459–60.

16. *Ibid.,* I, p. 471; Hazelton, *op. cit.,* p. 108.

17. See Document III; Hazelton, *op. cit.,* p. 99.

18. *Ibid.,* p. 118.

19. The manuscript of Dickinson's speech was discovered and edited by Dr. John H. Powell in 1941; *Pennsylvania Magazine of History and Biography,* LXV, p. 458–81.

20. Burnett, *op. cit.,* I, p. 526.

21. W. F. Dana, "The Declaration of Independence as Justification for Revolution," *Harvard Law Review,* XIII (Jan., 1900), p. 319–43.

22. Becker, *op. cit.,* xvii; Document VIII, page two.

23. Hazelton, *op. cit.,* p. 121.

24. *Ibid.,* p. 149–54.

25. *Ibid.,* p. 141.

26. From the original letter lent by the Massachusetts Historical Society to the Library of Congress; it was copied by a clerk and signed by Adams. Hazelton, *op. cit.,* p. 142–43.

27. That is, the Rough Draft, now in the Jefferson Papers in the Library of Congress; see Document V.

28. This copy, if made, is not known to be in existence.

29. Hazelton, *op. cit.,* p. 144.

30. *Ibid.,* p. 172 *ff.*

31. I am informed that the Adams Manuscripts contain an unpublished letter from John Adams to Cotton Tufts, the manager of his property, dated at Philadelphia June 23, 1776, the first paragraph of which reads as follows: "You mention Independence and Confederation. These things are now become objects of direct consideration. Days and Times, without number, have been spent upon these subjects, and at last a Committee is appointed to prepare, a Draught of Confederation, and a Declaration that these Colonies are free States, independent of all Kings, Kingdoms, Nations, People, or States in the World."

32. See Document II; W. C. Ford, "Jefferson's Constitution for Virginia," *The Nation,* LI, p. 107; *Writings of Jefferson,* P. L. Ford, ed., II, p. 7 *ff.*; Hazelton, *op. cit.,* p. 148; Marie Kimball, *op. cit.,* 289–90; John C. Fitzpatrick, *The Spirit of the American Revolution,* p. 2. Hazelton, *op. cit.,* p. 146–47. Only the first two of the six pages of Jefferson's proposed constitution are reproduced in Document II.

33. Hazelton, *op. cit.,* p. 148.

34. *Ibid.,* p. 451–52.

35. *Writings of Jefferson,* P. L. Ford, ed., I, p. 462*ff.*

36. The text in this clause of the Preamble is taken from Document II and that of the Declaration from Document IV; for a more detailed analysis of the parallel in phraseology, see Fitzpatrick, *op. cit.,* p. 5–6.

37. The draft of the Declaration of Rights appeared also in the *Pennsylvania Gazette* of June 12 as taken from Dixon and Hunter's *Virginia Gazette* of June 1.

38. *Writings of Jefferson,* P. L. Ford, ed., II, p. 42*ff.* The Rough Draft has been reproduced in facsimile several times; the Adams, Madison, Washburn, and Cassius F. Lee copies have never been reproduced in facsimile heretofore. Becker, *op. cit.,* p. 173, supposes that the copy in the Rough Journal is "the more authoritative text," though the Supreme Court of the United States has on occasion relied upon the engrossed copy as the official text. The text as given in *Revised Statutes of the United States,* 1878 ed., is from the Rough Journal.

39. *Op. cit.,* p. 140.

40. I have counted as a single alteration all additions or excisions involved in a single suggestion, as nearly as can be determined. For example, on page one of the Rough Draft, the clause "whenever any form of government shall become destructive of these ends" was altered by deleting "shall" and adding "s" to "become." This deletion and the necessary addition which it involved are counted as one alteration.

41. That is, eliminating the title and counting as first line that which begins "When in the course of human events …."

42. *Op. cit.,* p. 154.

43. Burnett, *op. cit.,* I, p. 500

44. Adams, indeed, stated in his *Autobiography* that Jefferson "took the Minutes [of the sub-committee] *and in a day or two* produced to me his Draught." If this is correct, Adams would have seen the Rough Draft while Franklin was at home ill. Charles Francis Adams thought that Jefferson had presented the Declaration to John Adams before showing it to Franklin. I join with Hazelton, *op. cit.,* p. 345, 348–49, 601, in concurring in this view. <A note from Jefferson to Franklin, dated [June 21?, 1776] led Boyd to speculate, finally, that Jefferson sent Franklin a draft of the Declaration on June 21; Boyd, *Papers,* I, 404–5.>

45. A comparison of this paragraph beginning "he has dissolved" as it appears in the first draft of the constitution for Virginia with the same paragraph in the second draft shows no verbal change as between the two; Ford, ed., *op. cit.,* II, p. 10. Yet in the corresponding paragraph in the Declaration there is considerable difference in the wording, as may be observed by comparing the text for this particular passage in the Adams copy (Document IV) and in Document II.

46. The one change that appears in this passage was made by Adams.

47. See Document VIII, page eight.

48. The title to Fitzpatrick's article in *Daughters of the American Revolution Magazine,* LV, p. 363*ff.*—"The manuscript from which Jefferson Wrote the Declaration of Independence"—is, in my view, somewhat misleading.

49. Becker, *op. cit.,* p. 154–56, thinks it likely that Adams suggested the substance of the paragraph (now partially obliterated) on the slip of paper which Jefferson pasted onto page two of the Rough Draft.

50. But Jefferson also wrote the following to John Vaughan, September 16, 1825: "Whenever, in the course of the composition, a copy became overcharged, and difficult to be read with amendments, I copied it fair, and when that also was crowded with other amendments, another fair copy was made &c. These rough drafts I sent to distant friends who were anxious to know what was passing …"; Hazelton, *op. cit.,* p. 345, and note 104 to Appendix.

51. Becker, *op. cit.,* p. 152

52. See Document VIII, page two. I have used the Madison copy for this comparison, since in it the changes are clearly marked by Jefferson himself, whereas in the Richard Henry Lee copy they were indicated by Arthur Lee. In consequence, a slight difference appears between my analysis and that of Mr. Becker, who followed the Lee copy.

53. A part of the slip (page two of the Rough Draft) on which this paragraph is written has been torn out and lost.

54. I feel quite certain in making the suggestion that "states" was not written by Jefferson. If he did write it, the beginning "s" in this word is the only one of

many in the entire Rough Draft formed in this manner. Moreover "states" as here written is quite different—especially in the base of the "t's"—from the same word as written ten other times in the Rough Draft; page one, line 30; page two, lines 13, 15 and 31 and the last word on the page two; lines 3, 18, 27, 32–33, and 35. I am inclined to believe that it is in the handwriting of John Adams. Fitzpatrick, p. 12–13, credits Franklin with the alterations detailed in (1), (4), (18), (19), and (26) in this stage. I am inclined to agree as to (1), (4)—though here Fitzpatrick errs in saying that "threaten" was struck out and "the" written above, whereas "threaten" was never in the Rough Draft—and perhaps (19). The alteration in (18) bears some resemblance to the hand of Adams.

55. In this passage Jefferson evidently made an error in drawing up the Madison copy by putting "new" before "officers"—Rough Draft, page two, line 24.

56. Becker, p. 164, indicates that this change was made before Adams took his copy, but it does not appear in that copy and so I have assigned it to this stage of the evolution of the text.

57. Becker, p. 165, implies that "colonies" was struck out before the draft went to Congress. But "states" is bracketed as a change made in Congress in the Rough Draft, in the Madison copy, and in the copy in Jefferson's *Notes*. In the Cassius F. Lee and Richard Henry Lee copies "colonies" appears to have been erased and "states" written over the erasure.

58. This phrase, "Scotch and other," may possibly have been inserted during the debates in Congress. It appears at this point in no copy except the Rough Draft. Thus it is probable that Jefferson, sitting in Congress, may have inserted it here since at line 17, page four, it was struck out by Congress. In a letter to Robert Walsh in 1818, Jefferson said that "the words 'Scotch and other foreign auxiliaries' excited the ire of a gentleman or two of that country." Now the phrase in these precise words "Scotch and other foreign"—"auxiliaries" is a misquotation—occurs only at line 8, page three in the Rough Draft. In the Richard Henry Lee and Cassius F. Lee copies, the words "Scotch and" are bracketed in the entire passage that was deleted. This warrants, I think, the supposition that someone objected to or at least pointed out the phrase before the whole passage was deleted, and Jefferson may have inserted it here at the time the whole paragraph was lost.

59. Instead of "others" the Madison copy and the copy in Jefferson's *Notes* indicate that "fellow-citizens" was the form originally given, but this is a change that was made by Congress.

60. Becker, p. 175, suggests that, as Adams was a member of the Committee whose duty it was to "superintend & correct the press," he may have influenced this change in spelling.

61. See Becker, p. 162n.

62. In making the Madison copy, Jefferson committed the error of inverting the change; Congress, according to this version, struck out "states" and inserted "colonies."

63. *Cf.* Becker, p. 166n.

64. The word "Parliament" occurs in the Virginia resolution of May 15 but not in the Lee Resolution of Independence.

65. Document VIII, page one.

66. Hazelton, *op. cit.,* p. 193-219.

A Declaration by the Representatives of the UNITED STATES OF AMERICA, in General Congress assembled.

When in the course of human events it becomes necessary for one people to dissolve the political bands which have connected them with another, and to assume among the powers of the earth the separate and equal station to which the laws of nature & of nature's god entitle them, a decent respect to the opinions of mankind requires that they should declare the causes which impel them to the separation.

We hold these truths to be self-evident; that all men are created equal & independent; that from that equal creation they derive rights inherent & inalienable, among which are the preservation of life, & liberty, & the pursuit of happiness; that to secure these ends, governments are instituted among men, deriving their just powers from the consent of the governed; that whenever any form of government shall becomes destructive of these ends, it is the right of the people to alter or to abolish it, & to institute new government, laying it's foundation on such principles & organising it's powers in such form, as to them shall seem most likely to effect their safety & happiness. prudence indeed will dictate that governments long established should not be changed for light & transient causes: and accordingly all experience hath shewn that mankind are more disposed to suffer while evils are sufferable, than to right themselves by abolishing the forms to which they are accustomed. but when a long train of abuses & usurpations [begun at a distinguished period